JAVASCRIPT

JAVASCRIPT BASICS
FOR BEGINNERS

Andy Vickler

Table of Contents

Introduction

This book contains proven steps and strategies on how to code in JavaScript. I have included in the book step-by-step programming techniques in JavaScript so that you can learn them properly. JavaScript is a scripted language. You will see a lot of script embedded in HTML tags. As JavaScript cannot work alone, I deemed it fit to embed it in HTML so that when you want to run it, it works well in web browsers.

If you want to practice what you have learned, you can open up a code editor, copy the code, and paste it in to check out the results. Also, you can simply load up the page to the web browser to see the results directly on the web page. Embedded scripts are in ready-to-work form. The best method to learn the scripts by heart and then edit them to customize them so that you can learn faster and in a fun way.

Whether you are making websites or are a student who aspires to become a web developer, or are planning to build a website for your own business, this book is the best literature you may come across on the market. Once you have gone through the first couple of chapters, you will be in the right mindset to move on and learn the complex topics. The best method is to go slow at first and pace yourself as the concepts become clearer.

Chapter One

An Introduction to JavaScript

JavaScript is an interpreted language. The definition of the language is broader than the word interpreted. You can define it as a procedural language that is weakly typed, based on prototypes, and is dynamic and imperative. JavaScript is developed and implemented in the form of a client-side programming language. It is a part of the web browser and is seen as something that can facilitate developers for the implementation of dynamic features and creation and integration of user interface on the web pages. You may find some implementation of JavaScript on the server-side as well. However, the popularity of the JavaScript programming language is largely based on its applications on the client-side. You may see applications of JavaScript outside of web applications as well. For example, you may find them being used as a way to add some interactivity to the desktop widgets and to documents in PDF format.

JavaScript was initially designed in the same mold as the C language was designed, but it also takes some Java programming language names. You should not mistake Java for JavaScript because the two are inherently different. They have different purposes and semantics as well.

The Developer of JavaScript

Brendan Each developed JavaScript initially with the name Mocha. The name was changed later on to LiveScript. Late on, it was changed again to JavaScript. The name confused some people, and it gave the impression that the new language, namely JavaScript, was an offshoot of Java. People thought that the new programing language was part of Netscape's marketing strategy to gain the much-needed prestige in the world of new programming languages.

The next year, Microsoft introduced a similar client-side language integrated into their famous Internet Explorer 3.0 browser. It named the language JScript to get away with brand problems. The term as it sounds and looks was perceived as so much similar to JavaScript; however, where it differed was that it could not be made 100% compatible with the specifications of ECMA.

In 1997, a proposal popped up to submit JavaScript to ECMA standards, and in June 1997, ECMA standards adopted it with the nametag ECMAScript. The programming language also won the ISO standard recommendation. JavaScript amassed high-rated popularity because of the way it adapted to the internet. That is the reason it became one of the most used programming languages across the planet.

The Use Cases of JavaScript

JavaScript is at work at the client-side of most of the webpages around the world. When you open a webpage, and it had changed from when you previously opened it, well, those changes could have been made using JavaScript. Let me tell you something interesting. Open a web page on your computer screen. Right-click on the web page and then click on View Source. You will see the word JavaScript inside the code of the page. Do not confuse HTML with JavaScript because you may find the two in the code of the page.

HTML is a markup language that allows developers to format the content and create a dynamic web page. You can turn the text into bold, create the boxes and tables of your choice, and add buttons and bullets to the page. However, JavaScript lets you alter the text, add pop-up messages, and validate the text you have entered through HTML coding. HTML and JavaScript walk side by side. Where JavaScript moves ahead of HTML is the way it makes the page dynamic and interactive. It will allow your users to click on certain elements and open new pages from the existing page.

You should learn JavaScript because it is very easy to implement. All you need is to put the code in an HTML document and then instruct the browser to run it. JavaScript works on many computers and operating systems, even when the systems are offline. With JavaScript's help, you can create responsive interfaces that refine user experience and offers extremely dynamic functionality.

JavaScript allows users to load up content in the form of a document whenever the user needs it, and that too without putting the web page into a reload. We call the process Ajax. JavaScript allows you to run a test for existing possibilities in the browser and then react accordingly. The process is known as defensive Scripting. JavaScript will fix any problems that emerge on your web pages. It will cover up the holes that exist in the browser support.

When we compare all that JavaScript can do for us with other programming languages for the web, we realize that it can do so much more. JavaScript is highly demanded and loved because it allows you to build complex applications without any hassle. You can build complex applications with Flash as well, but JavaScript is the best way to go because it is a web standard.

When it comes to the uses of JavaScript, the uses keep on changing. At first, JavaScript's interaction with a website was constricted to forming interaction and giving users feedback. However, it evolved with time, and now the uses are much more than how it started.

The use cases of JavaScript are changing with the change of times. Users need to change the tried, tested, and boring web interface of clicking on links, filling out information on a web page, and sending off a bunch of forms. They look at making the same processes more modern and user-friendly. JavaScript has enabled users to create a sign-up form that has the capacity to check if a username is already taken or is available. This prevents users from enduring page reload that can somewhat be highly frustrating. A search box shows you the more relevant and suggested results when you type something. It shows something that is based on your entries. The pattern is known as autocomplete - without JavaScript, that would not have been possible.

The information that needs to change after set times without any input from the user is possible with the help of JavaScript. JavaScript may attempt to fix layout issues. By using JavaScript, you may find the exact area and position of any element on your web page. You can calculate the dimensions of the window of your browser. By collecting and using this information, you may help prevent the overlap of elements and other related issues. Let us suppose you have a menu for different levels. You can prevent the overlap of the menu items and scroll-bars by checking out the space for the sub-menu. Perhaps the best way by which JavaScript can help you is to enhance the interface that HTML gives you.

Code is labeled as the text that forms programs. In many chapters of the books, you will find a lot of code. Reading and writing code, I must say, is an integral part of the process to learn and write programs.

Metaprogramming is considered a powerful technique that can enable you to write a set of programs. The advent of ES6 has further eased off the utilization of metaprogramming in the world of JavaScript programming. You can use proxies and other similar features. The proxies of ES6 tend to facilitate the redefinition of different operations in objects.

The <script> Tag

Let us talk about the symbol that is the most used tag in the book. All the JavaScript code is enclosed inside the <script> tags.

```
<!DOCTYPE html>
<html>
<body>

<p>JavaScript rests in the Body</p>

<p id="demo12"></p>

<script>
document.getElementById("demo12").innerHTML
= "This is your First JavaScript";
</script>

</body>
</html>
JavaScript Rests in the Body
This is your First JavaScript
```

The older type of JavaScript was written differently. It had the following format such as <script type = "text/javascript">.

There are functions in JavaScript that you can use to execute blocks of code. You may call a function when some kind of event occurs. An event can be defined as a click button. You can place any kind of script in an HTML document. You can place the scripts either in the <head> or in the <body> or in both of them. The example of using a script in the head is as under:

```
<!DOCTYPE html>
```

```
<html>
<head>
<script>
function FunctionUN() {

document.getElementById("demo34").innerHTML
= "I have changed the Paragraph.";
}
</script>
</head>
<body>

<p>You have seen the JavaScript in the
Head</p>

<p id="demo">This is a Paragraph.</p>

<button type="button"
onclick="FunctionUN()">Click Me</button>

</body>
</html>

You have seen the JavaScript in the Head
This is a Paragraph.
Click Me
```

When you click the button on the web browser, you will trigger an invocation of the function. You also can put the script inside the <body> of the HTML page. You will invoke this function when you click the button.

```
<!DOCTYPE html>
<html>
<body>
```

```
<p>This is A Web Page</p>
<p id="demo1">This is a Paragraph</p>
<button type="button"
onclick="FunctionZ()">Click Me</button>

<script>
function FunctionZ() {
  document.getElementById("demo1").innerHTML
= "I have changed the Paragraph.";
}
</script>

</body>
</html>

This is A Web Page
I have changed the Paragraph.
Click Me
```

Display

There are different methods to display JavaScript in web browsers. Programmers use different techniques for display purposes. The first method that I have used in the book is the document.getElementById(id) method. In the phrase, id refers to the element that defines the HTML document. The word innerHTML defines the content of HTML.

```
<!DOCTYPE html>
<html>
<body>

<p>This is going to be my First Web Page</p>
<p>This will be the First Paragraph.</p>
```

10

```
<p id="demo1234"></p>

<script>
document.getElementById("demo1234").innerHTM
L = 4567 + 36;
</script>

</body>
</html>
```

```
This is going to be my First Web Page
This will be the First Paragraph.
4603
```

The second method that you can use is the document.write() method. This also is a simple one. However, I have not created any script in the book by using this method except for this example to show you how it works:

```
<!DOCTYPE html>
<html>
<body>

<p>This is going to be my First Web Page</p>
<p>This will be the First Paragraph.</p>

<p id="demo1234"></p>

<script>
document.write (4567 + 36);
</script>

</body>
</html>
```

```
This is going to be my First Web Page
This will be the First Paragraph.
4603
```

If you use this method after loading the HTML page, you will lose all data because it will be deleted. Therefore, you should beware of the consequences if you make this mistake. Also, you can create a button with this method and test the HTML page. See the following example.

```
<!DOCTYPE html>
<html>
<body>

<p>This is going to be my First Web Page</p>
<p>This will be the First Paragraph.</p>

<button type="button"
onclick="document.write(335 + 6)">Click
me</button>

</body>
</html>

This is going to be my First Web Page
This will be the First Paragraph.
Click me
Another method is the window alert method.
<!DOCTYPE html>
<html>
<body>

<p>This is going to be my First Web Page</p>
<p>This will be the First Paragraph.</p>
```

```
<p id="demo1234"></p>

<script>
window.alert (4567 + 36);
</script>

</body>
</html>

This is going to be my First Web Page
This will be the First Paragraph.
```

The above-mentioned text will be seen on the browser. Each time you run the code, you will see the result of the mathematical calculation on an alert window on the top of the screen. The use of the window keyword is optional. As the window object in JavaScript is global, you may drop its use and still get the same result. The following code will deliver the same result.

```
<!DOCTYPE html>
<html>
<body>

<p>This is going to be my First Web Page</p>
<p>This will be the First Paragraph.</p>

<p id="demo1234"></p>

<script>
alert (4567 + 36);
</script>

</body>
</html>
```

Another method is the console.log() method. This method is used for debugging the code and then displaying the data.

```
<!DOCTYPE html>
<html>
<body>

<p>This is going to be my First Web Page</p>
<p>This will be the First Paragraph.</p>

<p id="demo1234"></p>

<script>
console.log (4567 + 36);
</script>

</body>
</html>
```

Values

In the world of computers, you will only see one thing that is data. You can read through the data, modify the data, and create new data. All this data is stored in the form of sequences that are fundamentally alike. Bits are two-valued things that are usually described as ones and zeros. If you rip open a computer, you will see that data takes multiple forms like low and high charge, weak or strong signal, or dull and shiny spots on a CD. A piece of discrete information may be reduced to a sequence of ones and zeros. As a result, they are represented as bits. You can express any number in the form of bits. The process is the same as that of the decimal number. However, instead of writing many digits, you only have two to produce the result.

So, what are values? Just imagine an ocean of bits. A typical modern computer contains about 30 billion bits in the working memory. The working memory is also known as volatile data storage. The non-volatile storage that belongs to the hard disk or stands equivalent to that has a couple of orders of magnitude. If you want to continue working with these quantities of bits without mixing up and confusing things, you must separate them into tiny chunks known as values. It must be kept in mind that values are created with bits, yet these values play multiple roles.

There is a type for each value that determines the role the value has to play. Some values are labeled as numbers, some as pieces of text, and some are known as functions. There is standard practice to create a value - you must invoke its name first. The practice is not only standard but also convenient. There is no need to collect the right building material for the values or right away pay for them. Call for one, and you will have one. This doesn't mean that the values will be created out of thin air. Each value needs some place to store itself. So, if you are looking forward to creating a lot of them, you must think about the storage procedure. However, this is not a problem if you are looking forward to not creating them simultaneously. When you are not using a value, it will be discarded by the computer system.

Numbers

Values of the number are numeric values. In a JavaScript code, you will write it as follows:

13

You will use that inside a program, and it is going to bring bit patterns for the number in the memory of your computer. JavaScript will use a fixed number of bits, 64 bits, for storing value for a single number. There are unlimited patterns that you may create with 64 bits. This means that the amount of different numbers that the system may represent is restricted. With the N decimal digits, you have the opportunity to represent the 10N numbers.

The memory of the computer used to be a lot smaller, and people had to use certain groups of 8 and 16 bits in order to represent the numbers. It had been easy to overflow some small numbers to end up along with a number that could not fit inside some bits. Times have changed. Even the computers that fit into our pockets have immense space to save whatever you need.

These bits store negative numbers, and one bit of them alludes to the sign of a single number. A bigger issue that you may witness is that non-whole numbers ought to be represented as well. In order to do this, you need to use some bits for storing the decimal point's position.

Arithmetic

The main point is that number is used in arithmetic. They are used in programming to perform arithmetic operations like addition and multiplications. The simple operations of multiplication and addition need at least two numbers to produce a third number. The + is the symbol for addition, while the * is the symbol for multiplication. Both symbols are known as operators. When you are programming, and you place an operator between two numbers, you start an arithmetic operation. You can use parenthesis to shuffle the order in which operators perform. For example, in normal circumstances, multiplications come first. But if you put an addition in parentheses, you change the order. Now the editor will run addition first.

```
(500 + 100) * 500
```

When operators appear without parenthesis, their application order is determined based on precedents.

Strings

Another idea that you must learn by heart before delving into the ocean of JavaScript programming is the concept of strings. JavaScript strings represent text. You can write them by enclosing any piece of text that you want to convert into a string inside quotes. See the following examples.

'I am looking at the sinking sun.'

"I am going to take a flight to Mars."

`The weather is balmy, as April has started.`

You can use single quotes, double quotes, and backticks, as I have displayed in the above-mentioned examples. Putt each quote at the start or at the end of the strings so that the code editor recognizes the text as strings. You can literally put anything inside the quotes, and JavaScript will turn it into a string. However, a few characters of language are difficult to turn. You might have thought about how you will put quotes inside quotes. The first near-to-impossible thing to enclose inside strings is including a new line. Newlines appear when you press enter on the keyboard. You can do that without escaping when you use backticks.

If you want to include unique characters to a string, you can use a backslash (\). A backslash indicates that the character that precedes that is packed up with a special meaning. The process is known as escaping the character. If backlash precedes a quote, it will not end the string, but it will be included in the string. If you insert an 'n' character following the backslash, it will be interpreted in the form of a newline. If you put a 't' after the backslash, it alludes to a tab character. See the example of the following string.

"I will reach the moon\n And I will travel onwards to Mars."

What you will see on the web page will look like the following:

I will reach the moon

And I will travel onwards to Mars.

You may come across a situation where you need a backslash inside a string just to be a backslash and not any special code. If two backslashes tend to follow each other, they will definitely collapse. Just one will be left in the value of the resulting string.

You have to model strings in the form of a series of bits so that they can exist on the computer. The way JavaScript executes it depends on Unicode standards. These standards tend to assign a specific number to each character that you need, including the characters from Arabic, Greek, Armenian, and Japanese. If you have a number for each character, your string will be described by a specific sequence of numbers. That is how JavaScript executes the code. Still, you may face some kind of complication. The representation of JavaScript uses 16 bits per element of the string. Unicode defines much more characters than this. Some characters like emoji consume two character positions.

One peculiar aspect of JavaScript strings is that you cannot divide them, subtract them, and multiply them. However, there is one operator that you can use on strings. You can use the + operator on JavaScript strings to concatenate them or, in simple words, combine them into a single whole. See the following example:

```
"I" + "am" + "going" + "to" + "Mars" + "."
```

Strings values have several associated functions that you can use to perform different operations. The strings that you write with single or double quotes behave in the same manner. The only difference in both kinds of strings is the use of escape characters in strings. When you write something in ${}, the result will come as computed, then converted into a string, and then included at the same position.

JavaScript Arrays

JavaScript arrays can be identified with the help of square brackets. The items of arrays are filled up inside of square brackets and are separated by commas. See how we can declare arrays.

```
<!DOCTYPE html>

<html>

<body>


<p>Learn JavaScript Arrays</p>


<p>The indices of JavaScript Arrays are zero-based. It means the
first item in an array is [0].</p>


<p id="array-demo"></p>


<script>
        var carsArray =
        ["Volkswagen","Honda","Toyota", "Suzuki"];

        document.getElementById("array-
        demo").innerHTML = carsArray[0];
        </script>

        </body>
        </html>
```

Learn JavaScript Arrays

The indices of JavaScript Arrays are zero-based. It means the first item in an array is [0].

Volkswagen

Chapter Two

JavaScript Variables

Let us start with an example.

- My profession is coding.

- My state is Texas, USA.

If you have read them, you have added this information to your brain that I am a coder, and I live in Texas, USA. In the above-mentioned pieces of texts, the words and phrases coding and Texas, USA work the same way as variables do in JavaScript. The terms like My Profession and My State refer to specific values. They have the same relationship with Coding and Texas, USA that values have in JavaScript with variables.

You can create a variable by writing var (for variable). You will follow it by the name that you have to assign to the variable. A variable takes a specific value when you create one. The name of a variable can be anything you like. It is up to you to decide how it should sound. The value of a variable may change. The facts of a variable can change.

JavaScript variables can be simply defined as containers used to store values in the form of data. In the following example, I will use three variables: a, b, and c and fill them up with different values.

```
<!DOCTYPE html>
<html>
<body>

<p>These are JavaScript Variables</p>

<p>In the following example, a, b, and c are
JavaScript variables.</p>

<p id="variable-demo"></p>

<script>
var a = 50;
var b = 16;
var c = a + b;
document.getElementById("variable-
demo").innerHTML =
"The value of c is: " + c;
</script>

</body>
</html>
```

```
These are JavaScript Variables
```

In the following example, a, b, and c are JavaScript variables.

```
The value of c is: 66
```

As this is the first example, you need to understand it well. First of all, the line demarcates the backend code and the frontend of

JavaScript. You can say that it demarcates what you write in the code editor and what you see on the web page. The h1 and p headings may appear different in the book than if you display them on a web page. That is because of the h1 and p settings of the word processor that I am using. They will work fine if you copy and paste the code in an editor and launch it on a web page. Moreover, this is how I will write the code embedded in HTML structure in the rest of the book because this is how you will write it when you create a website. You need HTML embedding to write scripts in JavaScript in order to get them read by the web browsers. In the example mentioned above, you can see that each variable has a variable to hold.

Instead of creating a single alphabet variable, I will now create variables that have full-word names.

```
<!DOCTYPE html>
<html>
<body>

<p>You are studying JavaScript Variables</p>

<p>In the following example, the variables
will have full-word names.</p>

<p id="variable-demo"></p>

<script>
var milkprice = 150;
var oilprice = 160;
var totalprice = milkprice + oilprice;
```

```
document.getElementById("variable-
demo").innerHTML =
"The value of totalprice is: " + totalprice;
</script>

</body>
</html>

You are studying JavaScript Variables
```

In the following example, the variables will have full-word names.

```
The value of totalprice is: 310
```

JavaScript Identifiers

JavaScript variables need to be given unique names so that they can be easily identified. These unique names are labeled as identifiers. Identifiers may be short names like a, b, c, or lengthy descriptive names like totalprice, milkprice, and oilprice. There are some naming rules for JavaScript variables. You can use these rules to minimize the chance of errors.

- Variables must not contain digits, letters, dollar signs, and underscores.

- Variables may start with $ sign.

- Variables are case sensitive, which makes 'a' different from 'A' variable.

- Variables must have a letter to start with.

- You cannot use JavaScript keywords as variables.

If you see an equal sign like '=' in JavaScript, you should not mistake it as the one that is used in algebra. It has a different purpose.

The information that variables store may be used later on in a program you create. Scripts are long, so variables make it easy to locate useful values. Variables facilitate repeat use of a value in the same code. Instead of remembering the value, you create a variable and fill it in with the value.

Datatypes

JavaScript variables may hold different types of information like digits and texts. Text values in programming are named text strings. JavaScript may hold different types of data. As I have already explained, strings must be written in single and double quotes, whichever suits you. You write numbers without quotes. If you use quotes for numbers, the browser will interpret it as a string.

```
<!DOCTYPE html>
<html>
<body>

<p>You are studying JavaScript Variables</p>

<p>I am defining JavaScript datatypes.</p>

<p id="variable-demo"></p>

<script>

var num = 5555555.889;
var novelist = "Charles Dickens";
```

```
var introduction = 'Charles Dickens wrote
melodramatic novels!';

document.getElementById("variable-
demo").innerHTML =
num + "<br>" + novelist + "<br>" +
introduction;
</script>

</body>
</html>
```

```
You are studying JavaScript Variables
I am defining JavaScript datatypes.
5555555.889
Charles Dickens
Charles Dickens wrote melodramatic novels!
```

Declaration of Variables

The process of declaration of a variable is, in fact, the process of creation of a variable. You might have noticed in the above examples that I used the keyword var before each variable. Without the var keyword, you cannot create a variable. Once you have declared a variable, the variable will have no value. You have to assign one to it just like I did in the examples. Here the equal sign = is used. You thrust the sign in between the name of the variable and the value.

The Undefined Variables

In different programs, you can often declare variables without a value. The value may be something that you can calculate or something that you can provide to it later on, like the user's input. A variable that you declare without a value carries an 'undefined' value. I will use one of the examples that I have already created and strip off the variables' value. Let us use the latest example so that you can understand better.

```
<!DOCTYPE html>
<html>
<body>

<p>You are studying JavaScript Variables</p>

<p>I am defining JavaScript's undefined
variables.</p>

<p id="variable-demo"></p>

<script>

var num;
var novelist;
var introduction;

document.getElementById("variable-
demo").innerHTML =
</script>

</body>
</html>

You are studying JavaScript Variables
I am defining JavaScript's undefined
variables.
```

Re-Declaration

It is possible that you have defined and declared a variable but later on change your mind and make it undefined by the process I just explained. So, will it make it undefined? The answer is 'N0.' Making it undefined after declaration will not make the variable lose its value.

```
<!DOCTYPE html>
<html>
<body>

<p>You are learning JavaScript Variables</p>

<p>This is JavaScript's undeclared
variables.</p>

<p id="variable-demo"></p>

<script>

var num = 5555.444;
var novelist = "Charles Lamb";
var introduction = "Charles Lamb wrote
beautiful humor.";

var num;
var novelist;
var introduction;

document.getElementById("variable-
demo").innerHTML =
num + "<br>" + novelist + "<br>" +
introduction;
</script>
```

```
</body>
</html>
```

You are learning JavaScript Variables
This is JavaScript's undeclared variables.
5555.444
Charles Lamb
Charles Lamb wrote beautiful humor.

Arithmetic

JavaScript, like other programming languages, allows you to do mathematical calculations. You can add numbers, produce results, and then forward the results to a variable for storage. In the code, you can use the operators like = and +.

```
<!DOCTYPE html>
<html>
<body>

<p>JavaScript Arithmetic</p>

<p>This is JavaScript's undeclared
arithmetic.</p>

<p id="variable-demo"></p>

<script>

var a = 15 + 3452 + 13 + 8 + 1;

document.getElementById("variable-
demo").innerHTML = a

</script>
```

```
</body>
</html>

JavaScript Arithmetic
This is JavaScript's undeclared arithmetic.
3489
```

Subtraction

The next arithmetic operator to be discussed is subtraction. The sign of the operator is the same as is used in algebra. You can fill up the program with the numbers of your choice and put the – sign in between to start the subtraction process.

```
<!DOCTYPE html>
<html>
<body>

<p>JavaScript Arithmetic</p>

<p>JavaScript subtraction.</p>

<p id="variable-demo"></p>

<script>

var a = 55;
var b = 40;
var c = a - b;

document.getElementById("variable-
demo").innerHTML = c
</script>

</body>
```

```
</html>

JavaScript Arithmetic
JavaScript subtraction.
15
```

JavaScript String Concatenation

Just like you learned to add numbers, JavaScript allows you to concatenate strings. I will use the + operator to join strings in the following example.

```
<!DOCTYPE html>
<html>
<body>

<p>JavaScript String Concatenation</p>

<p>JavaScript datatypes.</p>

<p id="variable-demo"></p>

<script>

var a = "Charles Dickens" + "" + " wrote" +
"" + " melodramatic novels!";

document.getElementById("variable-
demo").innerHTML = a
num + "<br>" + novelist + "<br>" +
introduction;
</script>

</body>
</html>
```

```
JavaScript String Concatenation
JavaScript datatypes.
Charles Dickens wrote melodramatic novels!
```

JavaScript Let Keyword

In JavaScript, the let keyword aims at the declaration of variables. The var keyword may also be used for the declaration of variables; however, the key difference is in the scope of the two. The var keyword is based on function scope, while the let keyword is based on block scope. Learning how to use the let keyword is connected to learning the difference between the var keyword and the let keyword.

Global Scope

The variables that you declare out of JavaScript functions.

```
<!DOCTYPE html>
<html>
<body>

<p>JavaScript Let Keyword</p>

<p>You can access a GLOBAL variable working
from any script or any function.</p>

<p id="let-demo"></p>

<script>
var cars = "BMW";
Function1();

function Function1() {
```

```
document.getElementById("let-
demo").innerHTML = "I plan to buy a " + cars
+ " for my daily commute and offroading.";
}
</script>

</body>
</html>

JavaScript Let Keyword
```

You can access a GLOBAL variable working from any script or any function.

I plan to buy a BMW for my daily commute and offroading.

You may access global variables from any point inside of a JavaScript program.

Function Scope

The variables you will declare in the limits of a JavaScript function bear Function Scope. In the following example, I will declare variables in the precincts of functions.

```
<!DOCTYPE html>
<html>
<body>

<p>These are JavaScript Scopes</p>

<p>I will define and declare a variable
outside of Function2().</p>

<p id="let-demo1"></p>
```

```
<p id="let-demo2"></p>

<script>
Function2();

function Function2() {
  var cars = "BMW";
  document.getElementById("let-
demo1").innerHTML = typeof cars + " " +
cars;
}
document.getElementById("let-
demo2").innerHTML = typeof cars;
</script>

</body>
</html>

These are JavaScript Scopes
```

I will define and declare a variable outside of Function2().

```
string BMW
undefined
```

I attempted to define the variables in and out of the function. So when I checked the types of the variables, I learned that the variable thrown out of the function limits was labeled as undefined. This is the reason we call them function scope variables. So, if you write a code and mistakenly drive a variable out of the function, you will see the same message. The solution is to include the declaration in the function brackets, and the code will start working fine.

Block Scope

The variables that you declare using the var keyword are void of Block Scope. Only the variables that you declare within the curly braces may be accessed from out of the block. Block Scope was introduced in JavaScript in ES2015. Before this period, it had no scope. While the variables with the var keyword do not have Block Scope, the variables that you declare using the let keyword can have Block Scope.

The var keyword, in some cases, creates problems for programmers. Especially when you attempt to redeclare a variable by including the var keyword, you will see a bunch of problems popping up in the editor. If you redeclare a variable within a block, you will also redeclare it out of the same block. This will cause additional problems in the long run.

```
<!DOCTYPE html>
<html>
<body>

<p>This code snippet will declare your
variable with the var keyword</p>

<p id="let-demo"></p>

<script>
var  xyz = 10000;
// You can see the value of xyz is 10000
{
   var xyz = 1;
   // Now the redeclared value of xyz
variable is 1
```

```
}
// See the redelared value of variable xyz
has been applied or not
document.getElementById("let-
demo").innerHTML = xyz;
</script>

</body>
</html>
```

This code snippet will declare your variable with the var keyword

```
1
```

So, you can see that we ran into a big problem. With the var keyword, redeclaration can be a hassle to grapple with. This is where the let keyword comes into play. It solves the problem of redeclaration. If you have used the let keyword to declare a variable, you will not have any problem when you redeclare the same variable. In the following code, I will explain how the let keyword solves the problem of redeclaration.

```
<!DOCTYPE html>
<html>
<body>

<p>I will use the let keyword now to
redeclare a variable</p>

<p id="let-demo"></p>

<script>
var  xyz = 1000;
// The value of xyz variable is 1000
{
```

```
    let xyz = 1;
    // Now the value of xyz is set at 1
}
// The let keyword will let the variable xyz
retain the previously declared value
document.getElementById("let-
demo").innerHTML = xyz;
</script>

</body>
</html>
```

I will use the let keyword now to redeclare a variable

```
1000
```

As the let keyword was introduced later, Internet Explorer 11 and the previous versions do not support it. Presently, Chrome 49, Firefox 44, Opera 36, Edge 12, and Safari 11 support the use of the let keyword.

Both var and let keywords have different behaviors when it comes to the use of JavaScript loops. See the following two examples to understand the difference between the two keywords.

Example 1

```
<!DOCTYPE html>
<html>
<body>

<p>The JavaScript let Keyword</p>

<p id="let-demo"></p>
```

```
<script>
var xyz = 4;
for (var xyz = 0; xyz < 9; xyz++) {

}
document.getElementById("let-
demo").innerHTML = xyz;
</script>

</body>
</html>
```

The JavaScript let Keyword

9

Example 2:

```
<!DOCTYPE html>
<html>
<body>

<p>The JavaScript let Keyword</p>

<p id="let-demo"></p>

<script>
let xyz = 4;
for (let xyz = 0; xyz < 9; xyz++) {

}
document.getElementById("let-
demo").innerHTML = xyz;
</script>

</body>
```

```
</html>
```

The JavaScript let Keyword

4

In the first example, when I used the var keyword, the variable declared within the loop redeclares the xyz variable from outside the loop. However, when I used the let keyword in example 2, the variable declared inside the loop did not redeclare the one outside of the loop. When you use let to declare xyz variable inside the for loop, you will only see the xyz variable in the loop and never out of that.

Both let keyword and var keyword aim at declaring variables. However, before you use them in creating JavaScript programs, you should understand the key differences between the two.

- The var keyword is largely used in older JavaScript versions, while the let keyword is considered the latest method to declare variables. You may say the ley keyword starts with ES6, which also is known as ES2015.

- The var keyword is basically function scoped while the let keyword is block scoped.

If we talk about what is recommended of the two keywords, we may say that the let keyword is the best option to consider when you are writing a program. However, some browsers do not support the let keyword. Therefore, you may feel the need to use the var keyword.

Chapter Three

JavaScript Constants

The const keyword in JavaScript was introduced in ES2015. The variables that are defined with the const keyword work as well as those that are defined with the let keyword. The only difference is that you cannot reassign them. Once you initialize a constant, you cannot change its value 0afterward. This is what makes constant different from the var keyword. If you have to declare a constant, you need to initialize it first.

You should think over for a while whether you have to use a constant or not in a program. You should only use it when you are sure that you will not have to change the value of the variable.

The name of a constant can be a legal identifier.

```
<!DOCTYPE html>
<html>
<body>

<p>You are learning JavaScript constants</p>
```

```
<p>Keep in mind that you cannot change
primitive values.</p>

<p id="const-demo"></p>

<script>
try {
  const xyz = 89.141592653589793;
  xyz = 54.14;
}
catch (err) {
  document.getElementById("const-
demo").innerHTML = err;
}
</script>

</body>
</html>
```

```
You are learning JavaScript constants
Keep in mind that you cannot change
primitive values.
TypeError: Assignment to constant variable.
```

Block Scope

The declaration of variables by using the const keyword is similar to the declaration by using the let keyword when you are using Block Scope. The following example will explain how it inclines toward the let keyword and distances itself from the var keyword.

```
<!DOCTYPE html>
<html>
<body>
```

```
<p>In this example, I will be declaring a
Variable by Using the const keyword</p>

<p id="const-demo"></p>

<script>
var  xyz = 15;
// The value of xyz is 15
{
   const xyz = 1;
   // The value of xyz is 1
}
// The value of xyz is 15
document.getElementById("const-
demo").innerHTML = xyz;
</script>

</body>
</html>
```

In this example, I will be declaring a Variable by Using the const keyword

```
15
```

Unlike a variable declared with the var keyword, constants must be assigned a value upon declaration. You cannot the value section empty. The word constant is a bit confusing, if not entirely misleading. The keyword const does not define constant values. In reality, it defines constant references to the values you use in the equation. That is why you cannot change the primitive values of constants. However, you can change properties.

Primitive Values

If you give a constant a primitive value, you will not be able to change the values later on.

```html
<!DOCTYPE html>
<html>
<body>

<p>These are JavaScript constants</p>

<p>Let try if we can change primitive
value.</p>

<p id="const-demo"></p>

<script>
try {
  const xyz = 5556.175757557757793;
  xyz = 3555.19090;
}
catch (err) {
  document.getElementById("const-
demo").innerHTML = err;
}
</script>

</body>
</html>
```

These are JavaScript constants

```
Let try if we can change primitive value.
TypeError: Assignment to constant variable.
```

While you cannot change the primitive values in JavaScript constants, you can change objects' properties. In the following example, I will create an object with the keyword const, and then I will introduce some changes to the properties of that object to see if I can change them. See the example to get an idea of how it is done.

```html
<!DOCTYPE html>
<html>
<body>

<p>JavaScript constants</p>

<p>You can change the properties of objects
after Declaring them:</p>

<p id="const-demo"></p>

<script>
// I am going to create an object:
const mycar = {name:"Honda", model:"Vezel",
make:"Japan", color:"Grey"};

// Let us Change the property:
mycar.model = "Civic";

// You also can add a new property:
mycar.transmission = "Automatic";

// It is time to display your properties:
document.getElementById("const-
demo").innerHTML = "I have a " + mycar.name
+ "." + " It is of " + mycar.color + " color
and its model label is " + mycar.model + ".
" + "This car has " + mycar.transmission +
".";
```

```
</script>

</body>
</html>
```

JavaScript Constants

You can change the properties of objects after Declaring them:

I have a Honda. It is of Grey color, and its model label is Civic. This car has Automatic.

You saw that I changed the model from Vezel to Civic. I also added new properties to describe the mode of transmission of the car. This facilitates programmers as they can create an object and then add or change properties as they deem fit as per changing needs. However, you cannot reassign a different object to the same constant in a program. If you do that, you will see an error.

```
<!DOCTYPE html>
<html>
<body>

<p>Learning JavaScript constants</p>

<p>Prohibited: You cannot reassign a
different object to the same constant:</p>

<p id="const-demo"></p>

<script>
try {
    const mycar = {name:"Honda",
model:"Vezel", make:"Japan", color:"black"};
```

```
    mycar = {name:"BMW", model:"Z1",
make:"German", color:"red"};
}
catch (err) {
    document.getElementById("demo").innerHTML
= err;
}
</script>

</body>
</html>
```

Learning JavaScript constants

Prohibited: You cannot reassign a different object to the same constant:

Constant Arrays

You can create arrays with the const keyword, and you can change them as well.

Chapter Four

Prompts and Conditionals

A prompt box is used to ask a user to provide information and give a response field for the answer. The code asks a user some questions and then offers answers in the respective field for a response. You can change the response. Whether you leave the default response as-is or change it to something else, your response will be assigned to a variable.

A prompt code is akin to an alert code. However, there are two differences. For a prompt code, you need to follow a method to receive a response from the user, which means that you need to start the code by the declaration of a variable. After that, you have to use an equal sign. In the prompt, you must specify a second string, which is the default response that pops up in the field when you see the display of the prompt. If a user leaves it as-is and instead clicks OK, your default response will shift to a variable. However, you have the option to declare a default response or not. You have the option to assigning the strings to a specific variable, and then you need to specify variables rather than strings within the parentheses.

Some programmers use the line window.prompt instead of simply writing prompt. This practice is formal and is considered the right way to write it. However, as everyone is short on time, most coders prefer to write prompt instead.

The JavaScript if Statement

In this section, I will explain how you have to deal with different types of conditions in the world of JavaScript. Let us suppose you have coded a prompt that asks users to provide the location where the American president presently lives. Here is the line that users see on display: "Where do you live?"

If a user answers correctly, you may display an alert that will congratulate him. To finish this task successfully, you are going to need the if statement. If the user gives the right answer by entering the White House, he will be congratulated by your program. If he enters something else, the program returns nothing. The code will not allow any other answer to the question.

An if statement, which I will include an example of later, starts with the keyword *if*. The space that will separate it from parenthesis is a must for the code. When you have written the if statement and also included the space, you need to create and fill up a variable with the correct answer to your question so that the if condition may test it. You have to enclose the condition inside parentheses. If the condition is true, there will be an alert or any other kind of action that you have directed the code to perform. The execution may be of one statement or multiple statements. The first line of the if statement ends with a curly bracket. An entire if statement concludes with curly brackets on the same line. This comes as an exception to a rule that a typical statement concludes with a semicolon. It is common for programmers to omit the semicolon when the statement is complex, paragraph-like, and has a curly bracket to the tail.

In some codes, you may also see a triple equal sign in if statements, and you may think that it is merely an equal sign. However, that's not the case. The equal sign is used to assign values to variables. If you are testing variables with values, you cannot use single equal signs. If you skip this step and use a single equal sign instead of a triple equal sign, your code will mess up. When the condition has been met, you may have multiple statements to execute.

Conditional statements have the inherent ability to perform multiple actions after testing different conditions. More often, when you write a code, you need to perform a bunch of actions for several decisions. There are different types of conditional statements that you may use in JavaScript. Here is a rundown of each of them. I will explain all of them one by one.

- The if keyword is used to specify a code, the editor must execute in case a condition stands true.

- The else keyword is used to specify a code that the editor must execute if the same condition stands false.

- The else-if keyword is used to put a new condition to test if the first condition ended up being false.

The if statement is case sensitive, so the keywords if and IF are two different words. If you replace if with IF, you will see an error on your screen.

```
<!DOCTYPE html>
<html>
<body>

<p>I will display "Have a Great Day!" if the
time is less than 15:00:</p>

<p id="if-demo">Have a Savory Evening!</p>

<script>
if (new Date().getHours() < 15) {
  document.getElementById("if-
demo").innerHTML = "Have a Great Day!";
}
</script>

</body>
</html>
```

I will display "Have a Great Day!" if the time is less than 15:00:

Have a Great Day!

The else Statement

You can use the else statement for the specification of code that needs to be executed if your condition pops up as false. I will use the same code and add the else statement to the code to see how we can use the else statement to extend our code and make it more

51

interactive and user-friendly. Now the user will have two options instead of the rigid one option code.

```html
<!DOCTYPE html>
<html>
<body>

<p>I would like you to click the button
given below to display a greeting as per the
current time:</p>

<button onclick="FunctionX()">Please hit me
to display the greetings</button>

<p id="ifelse-demo"></p>

<script>
function FunctionX() {
  var myhours = new Date().getHours();
  var mygreetings;
  if (myhours < 15) {
    mygreetings = "Have a Great Day";
  } else {
    mygreetings = "Have a Great Evening. I
hope you enjoy your dinner.";
  }
  document.getElementById("ifelse-
demo").innerHTML = mygreetings;
}
</script>

</body>
</html>
```

I would like you to click the button given below to display a greeting as per the current time:

Please hit me to display the greetings

Have a Great Day

You can see that the else statement integrated perfectly into the existing code. I have taken the liberty to add an interactive button to the code so that users may know exactly what to do. When a user hits the button, he will get a message that greets him. The message will be structured as per the time the program reads at your end. This is how you can build an interactive website app on your page and engage your visitors. Also, your visitors will love the way they will be welcomed.

The else if Statement

You can add the else-if statement to the code to specify the new condition if the first condition returns false. In the following example, I will add more than two conditions to see how they work and how much improvement they bring to our code.

```
<!DOCTYPE html>
<html>
<body>

<p>I would like you to click the button
given below to display a greeting as per the
current time:</p>
```

```
<button onclick="FunctionX()">Please hit me
to display the greetings</button>

<p id="ifelse-demo"></p>

<script>
function FunctionX() {
  var mygreetings;
  var mytime = new Date().getHours();
  if (mytime < 8) {
    mygreetings = "Have a Good Morning. I
hope you have had a nutritious breakfast.
Get ready for work";
  } else if (mytime < 15) {
    mygreetings = "Have a Great Day. Don't
forget to eat your lunch.";
  } else {
    mygreetings = "Have a Great Evening. Any
special plans for dinner?";
  }
  document.getElementById("ifelse-
demo").innerHTML = mygreetings;
}
</script>

</body>
</html>
```

I would like you to click the button given below to display a greeting as per the current time:

Please hit me to display the greetings

Have a Great Day. Don't forget to eat your lunch.

This worked perfectly. Now your program will display greetings messages all three times of the day. You can customize the message and make it more interactive as per the needs of your business. Some coders are in the habit of writing the if statements by removing the curly brackets. The practice is completely legal; however, it is a bit hard to do. Some programmers put the initial curly bracket on a new line. Another practice is to write the entire if statement on a single line, which is easier to do but difficult to read when you come back to study the structure of your program. I suggest that you follow the same rule as I have used in the above examples so that you find it easier to write and understand as well. You may use the double equal sign == in place of the triple equal sign in most cases. However, you may detect a bit of technical difference.

There are many formats to write the if statement and the variations of if statements as well. The possibilities of coding with the if statements are endless.

JavaScript Switch Statement

You can use the switch statement to perform different actions on JavaScript conditions. It will help you work on a single code block and execute it as well. The editor evaluates it once, runs a comparison among values, and in case of a match, it executes the block. In case of a mismatch, there will be no execution. The following program will run the switch statement through the program and comb your computer to see what day is on your computer calendar and what message the same day contains in the code. It will run the code through all seven days of the week, and when it reaches a match, it will run the message that you have already connected to the same day. See the following code.

```
<!DOCTYPE html>
<html>
<body>

<p id="switch-demo"></p>

<script>
var weekdays;
switch (new Date().getDay()) {
  case 0:
    weekdays = "the restful Sunday";
    break;
  case 1:
    weekdays = "the blue blue Monday";
    break;
  case 2:
    weekdays = "the superstitious Tuesday";
    break;
  case 3:
    weekdays = "the hectic Wednesday";
    break;
  case 4:
    weekdays = "the overwhelming Thursday";
    break;
  case 5:
    weekdays = "the joyful Friday";
    break;
  case 6:
    weekdays = "the sleepy Saturday";
}
```

```
document.getElementById("switch-
demo").innerHTML = "Today is " + weekdays +
"." + " Have a great and productive day!";
</script>

</body>
</html>
```

Today is the superstitious Tuesday. Have a great and productive day!

In the above code example, you might have noticed the addition of the break keyword. When the code reaches the break keyword, it jumps out of the specific switch block. This jumping out of the switch block puts a stopper on the execution of the switch block. You do not necessarily insert the break keyword in the last case of the switch block. Include it or not; it will end anyway. If you exclude the break keyword from the switch block, the web browser will execute the immediate next case even if there is a mismatch in the values. So, be ready for an error if you skip the break keyword.

There is another keyword that you may add to the switch statement. It runs the code even if there is a mismatch.

```
<!DOCTYPE html>
<html>
<body>

<p id="switch-demo"></p>

<script>
var weekdays;
switch (new Date().getDay()) {
```

```
    case 0:
      weekdays = "it is the restful Sunday";
      break;
    case 1:
      weekdays = "it is the blue blue Monday";
      break;
    case 3:
      weekdays = "it is the hectic Wednesday";
      break;
    case 4:
      weekdays = "it is the overwhelming
Thursday";
      break;
    case 5:
      weekdays = "it is the joyful Friday";
      break;
    case 6:
      weekdays = "it is the sleepy Saturday";
      break;
    default:
      weekdays = "I am desperately waiting for
the weekend because I have planned a
vacation.";
    }
document.getElementById("switch-
demo").innerHTML = weekdays
</script>

</body>
</html>
```

I am desperately waiting for the weekend because I have planned a vacation.

You might be thinking that the default case can only be put in the last of the code. However, this is not true. You can insert it anywhere in the code, even at the start of the code. It will work well.

```
<!DOCTYPE html>
<html>
<body>

<p id="switch-demo"></p>

<script>
var weekdays;
switch (new Date().getDay()) {
   default:
    weekdays = "I am desperately waiting for
the weekend because I have planned a
vacation.";
    break;
  case 0:
    weekdays = "it is the restful Sunday";
    break;
  case 1:
    weekdays = "it is the blue blue Monday";
    break;
  case 3:
    weekdays = "it is the hectic Wednesday";
    break;
  case 4:
    weekdays = "it is the overwhelming
Thursday";
    break;
  case 5:
    weekdays = "it is the joyful Friday";
    break;
  case  6:
    weekdays = "it is the sleepy Saturday";
```

```
}
document.getElementById("switch-
demo").innerHTML = weekdays
</script>

</body>
</html>
```

I am desperately waiting for the weekend because I have planned a vacation.

Chapter Five

JavaScript Strings and Arrays

I have already explained what strings are and how you can use them in your scripts. There are some methods that you can use when you are working with strings. Some primitive values cannot have methods or properties because they are not objects. However, JavaScript allows primitive values to have properties and methods because it treats primitive values like objects when executing properties and methods. You can learn the length of a string you are using in a program.

```
<!DOCTYPE html>
<html>
<body>

<p>Learning Properties of JavaScript
Strings</p>

<p>This String property will answer the
question about the length of your
string:</p>

<p id="string-demo"></p>
```

```
<script>
var msgX = "I am about to leave for New York
to start my own business.";
var msgY = msgX.length;
document.getElementById("string-
demo").innerHTML = msgY;
</script>

</body>
</html>
```

Learning Properties of JavaScript Strings

This String property will answer the question about the length of your string:

```
58
```

Another JavaScript method helps you hunt down a string within a string. The method I will use here is called indexOf(). If you have specified a string inside another string, you will have it found out for you. An important note to remember is that you can create another string inside a string by using single quotes. The following example will explain the procedure to do that.

```
<!DOCTYPE html>
<html>
<body>

<p>Learning Properties of JavaScript
Strings</p>
```

```
<p>This String property will answer the
question about the inner string of your
string:</p>

<p id="string-demo"></p>

<script>
var msgX = "I am about to leave for 'New
York' to start my own business.";
var msgY = msgX.indexOf("New York");
document.getElementById("string-
demo").innerHTML = msgY;
</script>

</body>
</html>
```

This String property will answer the question about the length of your string:

```
25
```

You can see the index of the inner string has been displayed on the screen. Please remember that JavaScript counts the index number from point zero.

The lastIndexOf() Method

You can use the lastIndexOf() method to see the index of final occurring of New York, which is our specified inner string.

```
<!DOCTYPE html>
<html>
<body>
```

```
<p>Learning Properties of JavaScript
Strings</p>

<p>This String property will answer the
question about the inner string of your
string:</p>

<p id="string-demo"></p>

<script>
var msgX = "I am about to leave for 'New
York' to start my own business.";
var msgY = msgX.lastIndexOf("New York");
document.getElementById("string-
demo").innerHTML = msgY;
</script>

</body>
</html>
```

This String property will answer the question about the inner string of your string:

```
25
```

What If the Index Is Not Found?

If the methods fail to find the index, they will return -1. This may happen if you write the wrong spelling or a completely different word in the code.

```
<!DOCTYPE html>
<html>
<body>
```

```
<p>Learning Properties of JavaScript
Strings</p>

<p>This String property will answer the
question about the inner string of your
string:</p>

<p id="string-demo"></p>

<script>
var msgX = "I am about to leave for 'New
York' to start my own business.";
var msgY = msgX.lastIndexOf("Washington");
document.getElementById("string-
demo").innerHTML = msgY;
</script>

</body>
</html>
```

This String property will answer the question about the inner string of your string:

```
-1
```

The search() Method

```
There is another method to locate the
specified inner string in a long string. You
can use the search() method for hunting it
down if the match is perfect.
<!DOCTYPE html>
<html>
<body>
```

```
<p>Learning Properties of JavaScript
Strings</p>

<p>This String property will answer the
question about the inner string of your
string:</p>

<p id="string-demo"></p>

<script>
var msgX = "I am about to leave for 'New
York' to start my own business.";
var msgY = msgX.search("New York");
document.getElementById("string-
demo").innerHTML = msgY;
</script>

</body>
</html>
```

This String property will answer the question about the inner string of your string:

25

If you notice the results of the two methods, namely search() and indexOf(), you will realize they are the same. They accept the same arguments and then respond with the same values. However, technically, the two methods are different a great deal. The search() method cannot take in a second starting position argument, while the indexOf() method cannot take in powerful search values.

Parts Extraction

You can break up a string into many parts as per the needs of your program. JavaScript gives us three methods to break up a string. The first method is labeled as the slice() method. It extracts one part of your string and displays the same in the form of a new string. You need to execute two parameters; one is the starting position of the string, and the other is the ending position of the string. See how you can do that.

```
<!DOCTYPE html>
<html>
<body>

<p>Learning Properties of JavaScript
Strings</p>

<p>This String property will answer the
question about the inner string of your
string:</p>

<p id="string-demo"></p>

<script>
var msgX = "I am about to leave for 'New
York' to start my own business.";
var msgY = msgX.slice(23, 34);
document.getElementById("string-
demo").innerHTML = msgY;
</script>

</body>
</html>
```

This String property will answer the question about the inner string of your string:

```
'New York'
```

Please keep in mind that JavaScript counts the index from the 0 point. If one parameter turns out to be negative, you have to count it from the string's ending point. It will slice the string backward. You can try it out and get the result. I will skip it for now and test what happens if you forget to insert the ending point.

```
<!DOCTYPE html>
<html>
<body>

<p>Learning Properties of JavaScript
Strings</p>

<p>This String property will answer the
question about the inner string of your
string:</p>

<p id="string-demo"></p>

<script>
var msgX = "I am about to leave for 'New
York' to start my own business.";
var msgY = msgX.slice(23);
document.getElementById("string-
demo").innerHTML = msgY;
</script>

</body>
</html>
```

This String property will answer the question about the inner string of your string:

'New York' to start my own business.

You can see that it has displayed the rest of the text to the end. If the starting point is negative and the ending point is missing, you will see the results being counted from the end to the slicing point.

The second method to cut the string and make a substring is the substring() method. This is as simple as the slice method is. Where it differs is its unacceptance of negative indices. See the following example to understand its use.

```
<!DOCTYPE html>
<html>
<body>

<p>Learning Properties of JavaScript
Strings</p>

<p>This String property will answer the
question about the inner string of your
string:</p>

<p id="string-demo"></p>

<script>
var msgX = "I am about to leave for 'New
York' to start my own business.";
var msgY = msgX.substring(23, 34);
document.getElementById("string-
demo").innerHTML = msgY;
</script>
```

```
</body>
</html>
```

This String property will answer the question about the inner string of your string:

```
'New York'
```

The third and last slicing method is the substr() method, which is quite similar to slice(). The second parameter defines the length of the rest of the sliced string.

```
<!DOCTYPE html>
<html>
<body>

<p>Learning Properties of JavaScript
Strings</p>

<p>This String property will answer the
question about the inner string of your
string:</p>

<p id="string-demo"></p>

<script>
var msgX = "I am about to leave for 'New
York' to start my own business.";
var msgY = msgX.substr(23, 34);
document.getElementById("string-
demo").innerHTML = msgY;
</script>

</body>
```

```
</html>
```

This String property will answer the question about the inner string of your string:

```
'New York' to start my own business
```

JavaScript gets interesting when it allows you to replace values inside of a string. For example, the string I have included in my examples contains New York as the city that I will be visiting. JavaScript allows you to change the name of the city instead of writing a new code and creating a new string. This saves a lot of your time when you are creating lengthy programs. The method can be identified as replace().

```
<!DOCTYPE html>
<html>
<body>

<p>Learning Properties of JavaScript
Strings</p>

<p id="string-demo"></p>

<script>
var msgX = "I am about to leave for 'New
York' to start my own business.";
var msgY = msgX.replace('New York', 'Las
Vegas');
document.getElementById("string-
demo").innerHTML = msgY;
</script>

</body>
```

```
</html>
```

Learning Properties of JavaScript Strings

I am about to leave for 'Las Vegas' to start my own business.

By default, JavaScript replace() will not work if you write NEW YORK instead of New York. It is case sensitive, and it identifies a different case as a different word. Therefore, if you find out that the method is not working, better check out the case of the words. Also, the replace() method only replaces the first match. If there is more than one New York in the string, it will only replace the first match and leave out the rest of the words intact. If you want to use capital case despite the warning, you have to use a regular expression such as /i with the word to enable the browser to recognize the match. The regular expression will make the word insensitive. See how you should write it in the editor.

```
<!DOCTYPE html>
<html>
<body>

<p>Learning Properties of JavaScript
Strings</p>

<p id="string-demo"></p>

<script>
var msgX = "I am about to leave for 'New
York' to start my own business.";
var msgY = msgX.replace(/NEW YORK/i, 'Las
Vegas');
```

```
document.getElementById("string-
demo").innerHTML = msgY;
</script>

</body>
</html>
```

Learning Properties of JavaScript Strings

I am about to leave for 'Las Vegas' to start my own business.

Let us see what the code will look like if you miss out on the regular expression and still use the capital case in the code.

```
<!DOCTYPE html>
<html>
<body>

<p>Learning Properties of JavaScript
Strings</p>

<p id="string-demo"></p>

<script>
var msgX = "I am about to leave for 'New
York' to start my own business.";
var msgY = msgX.replace('NEW YORK', 'Las
Vegas');
document.getElementById("string-
demo").innerHTML = msgY;
</script>

</body>
</html>
```

Learning Properties of JavaScript Strings

I am about to leave for 'New York' to start my own business.

You can see that the code does not work anymore.

Go Global

I have already explained that if you have to replace more than one word, you cannot do that by the replace method. It just does not work. However, there is a solution to the problem. If you have more than one words that must be replaced with another word, you need to use a regular expression again. This time the regular expression is labeled as /g. The method of including the expression is the same as that of /i. However, I will write a new string and include the expression so that you can understand it well.

```
<!DOCTYPE html>
<html>
<body>

<p>Learning Properties of JavaScript
Strings</p>

<p id="string-demo"></p>

<script>
var msgX = "The Coach of the NBA team will
visit Las Vegas. Las Vegas has a huge fan
base for NBA stars.";
var msgY = msgX.replace(/Las Vegas/g, 'Los
Angeles');
document.getElementById("string-
demo").innerHTML = msgY;
```

```
</script>

</body>
</html>
```

Learning Properties of JavaScript Strings

The Coach of the NBA team will visit Los Angeles. Los Angeles has a huge fan base for NBA stars.

There are some additional methods to tune up strings as well. You can convert a string into upper and lower cases by simple methods.

```
<!DOCTYPE html>
<html>
<body>

<p>I am converting strings into upper and
lower cases:</p>

<button onclick="FunctionX()">You need to
Hit me</button>

<p id="string-demo">JavaScript makes your
webpages interactive and user-friendly!</p>

<script>
function FunctionX() {
  var msg = document.getElementById("string-
demo").innerHTML;
  document.getElementById("string-
demo").innerHTML = msg.toUpperCase();

}
</script>
```

```
</body>
</html>
```

I am converting strings into upper and lower cases:

You need to Hit me

JavaScript makes your webpages interactive and user-friendly!

The above result is displayed when you run the code. Now I will click the button I have just created. You will see the results in the upper case. I will only display the results.

I am converting strings into upper and lower cases:

You need to Hit me

JAVASCRIPT MAKES YOUR WEBPAGES INTERACTIVE AND USER-FRIENDLY!

You can use the other method toLowerCase() to convert the text into lower case. Just replace toUpperCase() with toLowerCase().

The Concatenation

Concatenation is an integral part of almost all programming languages. Whenever there is a need to pair up two or more strings, programmers seek support from concatenation. It is the easiest method to join two more strings. The concat() method works smoothly if you have written the lines of code well. The most important things to care about are the placement of commas and whitespaces. The concat() method is used in place of the plus operator. There is no difference in the function—the two work as alternatives only. The following exercise will help you sail through the process of concatenation.

```
<!DOCTYPE html>
<html>
<body>

<p>Learnig JavaScript Strings</p>

<p id="string-demo"></p>

<script>
var msg1 = "I have been promoted as Chief
Executive Officer of Skyfall.";
var msg2 = "I will call a board meeting next
week.!";
var msg3 = msg1.concat(" ", msg2);
document.getElementById("string-
demo").innerHTML = msg3;
</script>

</body>
</html>
```

Learning JavaScript Strings

I have been promoted as Chief Executive Officer of Skyfall. I will call a board meeting next week.!

Almost all string methods have a habit of creating a new string, keeping the original string intact. They make a copy first and introduce the changes you suggest to the editor. Programmers say that strings can only be replaced. They cannot change.

Each day there have been efforts by programmers to introduce some new things to programming languages. The ECMAScript 2017 introduced more methods to JavaScript strings. The methods padStart and padEnd are now being used at the start and end of JavaScript strings.

String Arrays

The heading may appear a bit confusing. There is no such thing as string arrays. However, there is a new method that turns a string into an array.

```
<!DOCTYPE html>
<html>
<body>

<p>Please click "Click me" to produce the
first array element.</p>

<button onclick="FunctionX()">Click This
Button</button>

<p id="string-demo"></p>

<script>
function FunctionX() {

   var msg1 = "Texas, Las Vegas, Los
Angeles.";
   var msg2 = msg1.split(",");
   document.getElementById("string-
demo").innerHTML = msg2[0];
}
</script>
```

```
    </body>
    </html>
```

Please click "Click me" to produce the first array element.

```
    Click This Button
    Texas
```

Strings are amazing, and they can help you in your programming ventures a great deal if you learn well the methods and properties. JavaScript programming is the easiest and the most flawless of all programming languages if you have a great eye for nuances.

JavaScript Arrays

Just like variables, JavaScript Arrays, too, are containers of values. However, they deviate from the properties of variables in the sense that they can hold more data than a variable in one name. So, whenever you need to load up more data in the same name, you should use arrays. There is more than one way to set up an array. The easiest of them is to use the var keyword, then write the name of the arrays, and give values. An array holds individual values in one variable. You have to separate them by comma and put them all inside square brackets. The equal sign must follow the name of the variable.

When you have to access all the array values, you should use the index number just as you did in the strings. The number between the square brackets indicates the index. The number must correspond to the position of values in an array. The most important thing to remember is that the position of the index starts at 0.

When you have created an array, you are good to go and run it in the web browser. You should be able to see the requisite value on the screen of your browser. You can edit the index number and insert something else to display a different value. Save the edited number and refresh the browser to change the results. If your array has three items and you put in the number 3 for the index, you will see that the browser will display the word 'undefined' on the computer screen. This happened because you had only three items in the array. When you typed 3 for the index, you attempted to display the fourth item which was not there. Rather than displaying errors, JavaScript adds a new position in the array, which is not yet defined. JavaScript adds the new position to the end of the array. It remains undefined until you fill it up with a reasonable value. You can use the new undefined position to store data as per your needs.

```
<!DOCTYPE html>
<html>
<body>

<p>Learning JavaScript Arrays</p>

<p id="array-demo"></p>

<script>
var carsforsale = ["Honda", "Toyota", "GTX",
"Ford"];
document.getElementById("array-
demo").innerHTML = carsforsale;
</script>

</body>
</html>
```

Learning JavaScript Arrays

Honda,Toyota,GTX,Ford

You can see in the above-mentioned example that an array in JavaScript is a special kind of variable that holds multiple values at the same time. If you have a list of cars that you otherwise might have stored in multiple variables, you can use an array instead to pack it up with all the values and insert them in a web page. If you stored them in independent variables, you would have created four variables with different names. Now that's 4 cars, so you might think it is not a big deal to create four independent variables for these values. However, if you have 4000 values, it will be a problem to create independent variables for all of them. In this situation, the array comes to help. Similarly, if you have a hundred values and you must use them in a loop, independent variables will not help a great deal. Arrays are easier to work with because you can easily loop through them.

Spaces or line breaks are not of much importance in JavaScript arrays. You can write them in different formats. See the following example, which has the same content as above but a different format.

```
<!DOCTYPE html>
<html>
<body>

<p>Learning JavaScript Arrays</p>

<p id="array-demo"></p>
```

```
<script>
var carsforsale = ["Honda",
    "Toyota",
    "GTX",
    "Ford"];
document.getElementById("array-
demo").innerHTML = carsforsale;
</script>

</body>
</html>
```

Learning JavaScript Arrays

Honda,Toyota,GTX,Ford

It has the same result as the previous example. There is another method to create an array. This is called the JavaScript keyword 'new.' I will create an array by using the keyword new in the example given below.

```
<!DOCTYPE html>
<html>
<body>

<p>Learning JavaScript Arrays</p>

<p id="array-demo"></p>

<script>
var carsforsale = new Array("Honda",
"Toyota", "GTX", "Ford");
document.getElementById("array-
demo").innerHTML = carsforsale;
```

```
</script>

</body>
</html>
```

Learning JavaScript Arrays

Honda,Toyota,GTX,Ford

Let us analyze this new format and understand what is different in this. The first difference is the addition of the keyword new to the start of the array and right after the equal sign, followed by the keyword Array immediately next to the keyword New. Another prominent difference is the removal of square brackets and the addition of parentheses, but both methods work the same way. The second method is more complicated and extended. For the sake of simplicity, speed, and readability, you should opt for the first method that also is known as the array literal method.

Index Numbers

You can access the items of the arrays by using the index number. As already mentioned, the index for the array starts at number 0. In the following example, I will access the element that has the zero index.

```
<!DOCTYPE html>
<html>
<body>

<p>Learning JavaScript Arrays</p>

<p id="array-demo"></p>
```

```
<script>
var carsforsale = new Array("Honda",
"Toyota", "GTX", "Ford");
document.getElementById("array-
demo").innerHTML = carsforsale[0];
</script>

</body>
</html>
```

Learning JavaScript Arrays

```
Honda
```

Index numbers are helpful in the sense that they can aid in changing the values of the elements of the array. You can replace almost all elements of the array just by mentioning the index numbers.

```
<!DOCTYPE html>
<html>
<body>

<p>Learning JavaScript Arrays</p>

<p id="array-demo"></p>

<script>
var carsforsale = new Array("Honda",
"Toyota", "GTX", "Ford");
carsforsale[0] = "BMW"
carsforsale[1] = "Mitsubishi"
document.getElementById("array-
demo").innerHTML = carsforsale;
</script>
```

```
</body>
</html>
```

Learning JavaScript Arrays

```
BMW,Mitsubishi,GTX,Ford
```

Arrays are considered special objects. If you use the typeof operator to check the type of arrays, you will get the word 'object' in return. But we must stick to the word arrays to describe JavaScript arrays. The reason is that JavaScript arrays use numbers for accessing elements and objects use names of the items to give you access to the same items.

You can assign any value to an array. Whatever you can assign to a variable, you can assign to an array. You can mix up different types in the same arrays. Programmers more often prefer to give plural names to arrays like cities, countries, numbers, etc. The reason is that each array is a list of more than one item. Just like ordinary variables, you may declare one array only once.

JavaScript variables may be dubbed as objects, while JavaScript arrays are dubbed as special objects because an array may contain different kinds of variables. You can fill up an array with objects, functions, and even arrays. Just like strings, the real strength of arrays is because of their rich properties and built-in methods.

Array Properties

The first property to discuss is the length property. It returns the full length of an array, which contains all the elements of the array.

```
<!DOCTYPE html>
<html>
<body>

<p>Learning JavaScript Arrays</p>

<p id="array-demo"></p>

<script>
var carsforsale = new Array("Honda",
"Toyota", "GTX", "Ford");
document.getElementById("array-
demo").innerHTML = carsforsale.length;
</script>

</body>
</html>
```

Learning JavaScript Arrays

4

You can build a loop through the items of an array to display all of them or use all of them in a program. One of the most common methods for creating a loop is the for loop.

```
<!DOCTYPE html>
<html>
<body>

<p>These are JavaScript Arrays</p>

<p>I will use the for loop in the following
code</p>

<p id="array-demo"></p>
```

```
<script>
var carsforsale, msg, cLn, y;
carsforsale = ["BMW", "Mitsubishi", "Honda",
"Toyota"];
cLn = carsforsale.length;

msg = "<ul>";
for (y = 0; y < cLn; y++) {
  msg += "<li>" + carsforsale[y] + "</li>";
}
msg += "</ul>";

document.getElementById("array-
demo").innerHTML = msg;
</script>

</body>
</html>
```

These are JavaScript Arrays

I will use the for loop in the following code

- BMW

- Mitsubishi

- Honda

- Toyota

You have seen how you can display a neat and clean list of items on a web page. All the items of the array are displayed neatly in the form of bullet points. Next time you see a similar-looking list on a web page, you should know that it is the array and the for loop that did the wonder. There is another function to create the same effect in an array.

```
<!DOCTYPE html>
<html>
<body>

<p>These are JavaScript Arrays</p>

<p>I will use the for loop in the following
code</p>

<p id="array-demo"></p>

<script>
var carsforsale, msg;
carsforsale = ["BMW", "Mitsubishi", "Honda",
"Toyota"];


msg = "<ul>";
carsforsale.forEach(FunctionX);
msg += "</ul>"
document.getElementById("array-
demo").innerHTML = msg;

function FunctionX(value) {
   msg += "<li>" + value + "</li>";
}
</script>

</body>
</html>
```

These are JavaScript Arrays

I will use the for loop in the following code

- BMW

- Mitsubishi

- Honda

- Toyota

Adding Elements

You can add elements to an array by using the push() method. This JavaScript feature helps a great if you are working a retail firm and you have to upload new elements to the same array each day. JavaScript is amazing in the sense that it allows you to declare a variable with no values. After that, you can use the append function to add values to the same. You can change the values as well as per your shifting needs. All this may happen in one array.

```
<!DOCTYPE html>
<html>
<body>

<p>Learning JavaScript Arrays</p>

<p>I will use the push method to append new
elements to existing arrays.</p>

<button onclick="FunctionXX()">Please click
this Button</button>
```

```
<p id="array-demo"></p>

<script>
var veggies = ["Pumpkin", "Tomato",
"Ginger", "Potato"];
document.getElementById("array-
demo").innerHTML = veggies;

function FunctionXX() {
  veggies.push("Spinach");
  document.getElementById("array-
demo").innerHTML = veggies;
}
</script>

</body>
</html>
```

Learning JavaScript Arrays

I will use the push method to append new elements to existing arrays.

Please click this Button

Pumpkin, Tomato, Ginger, Potato

You will see the above result when you run the code in the browser. When you click on the button in the web browser, you will be able to see the newly appended element in the list of array items. When I click the button, I see the following result.

Please click this Button

Pumpkin, Tomato, Ginger, Potato,Spinach

You can manipulate the length property to append a new element to your array. See how you can use the length property.

```
<!DOCTYPE html>
<html>
<body>

<p>Learning JavaScript Arrays</p>

<p>I will use the push method to append new
elements to existing arrays.</p>

<button onclick="FunctionXX()">Please click
this Button</button>

<p id="array-demo"></p>

<script>
var veggies = ["Pumpkin", "Tomato",
"Ginger", "Potato"];
document.getElementById("array-
demo").innerHTML = veggies;

function FunctionXX() {
  veggies[veggies.length] = ("Spinach");
  document.getElementById("array-
demo").innerHTML = veggies;
}
</script>

</body>
</html>
```

Learning JavaScript Arrays

I will use the push method to append new elements to existing arrays.

Please click this Button

Pumpkin, Tomato, Ginger, Potato, Spinach

Arrays can be tricky to work with if you do not know what you are doing. For example, you can use the index number to append an element to an array. In the process, if you include a higher index to the code, you will create holes in the array that will be completely undefined.

```
<!DOCTYPE html>
<html>
<body>

<p>Learning JavaScript Arrays</p>

<p>I will add elements that have high
indices. The result will be undefined
"holes" in the array.</p>

<p id="undefinedarray-demo"></p>

<script>
var veggies, msg, cLn, XX;
veggies = ["Pumpkin", "Ginger", "Tomato",
"Garlic"];
veggies[8] = "Spinach";

cLn = veggies.length;
```

```
msg = "";
for (XX = 0; XX < cLn; XX++) {
    msg += veggies[XX] + "<br>";
}
document.getElementById("undefinedarray-
demo").innerHTML = msg;
</script>

</body>
</html>
```

Learning JavaScript Arrays

I will add elements that have high indices. The result will be undefined "holes" in the array.

Pumpkin

Ginger

Tomato

Garlic

undefined

undefined

undefined

undefined

Spinach

You can see that JavaScript does not return an error in the code. It just creates an undefined slot in the position that does not have an item to fill in. The undefined slot can be filled up with items if you need to later on. So, this cannot actually be called a fatal error.

Associative Arrays

In the world of programming, many programming languages have arrays that have named indices. The arrays that contain named indexes are labeled as associative arrays. Some programmers also label them as hashes. JavaScript has no support for the arrays that have named indexes. Arrays in JavaScript use numbered indexes.

```
<!DOCTYPE html>
<html>
<body>

<p id="array-demo"></p>

<script>
var car = [];
car[0] = "BMW";
car[1] = "Germany";
car[2] = 2018;
document.getElementById("array-
demo").innerHTML =
car[0] + " " + car[1] + " " + car[2];
</script>

</body>
</html>
```

BMW Germany 2018

There is a basic difference between JavaScript arrays and JavaScript objects. I already explained that arrays are numbered while objects are named. Now I will explain where you should use arrays and where you should use objects. As for JavaScript objects, you have to use it when you want the elements to be named as strings which are in the form of text. As for the arrays, you should use them where you must name the elements in numbers. If you switch positions, you will get unexpected results in the web browser.

Array Conversion

JavaScript has methods that allow you to convert an array into a string that is separated by commas. The method is known as the toString() method. I will use the example of veggies array and add the toString() method to the same, and the results will be visible in the web browser.

```
<!DOCTYPE html>
<html>
<body>

<p>Learning JavaScript Arrays</p>
<p id="undefinedarray-demo"></p>

<script>
var veggies = ["Pumpkin", "Ginger",
"Tomato", "Garlic"];
document.getElementById("undefinedarray-
demo").innerHTML = veggies.toString();
</script>

</body>
</html>
```

Learning JavaScript Arrays

```
Pumpkin, Ginger, Tomato, Garlic
```

You can see that the array has been converted into a string. There is not a neatly displayed list on the web page. Instead, you can see a jumbled-up list of items that are separated by commas. Not only does the toString() method converts an array into a string, but the join() method also does the same. It joins all the elements into a single whole. This method, too works as fine as the toString() method. The only difference is that this method allows you to specify a separator.

```
<!DOCTYPE html>
<html>
<body>

<p>Learning JavaScript Arrays</p>

<p id="array-demo"></p>

<script>
var veggies = ["Pumpkin", "Ginger",
"Tomato", "Garlic"];
document.getElementById("array-
demo").innerHTML = veggies.join(" - ");
</script>

</body>
</html>
```

Learning JavaScript Arrays

```
Pumpkin - Ginger - Tomato - Garlic
```

You can see that everything worked the same as with the toString() method. However, the code showed flexibility when it allowed me to choose the sign of my choice to separate the converted string elements. I have chosen " – " for the separation. However, you can choose other signs like * or +, whatever suits you.

Popping Arrays

When you are working with arrays to operate a retail outlet or a financial firm, you can use popping and pushing methods to extract or add elements. Popping flips off an element out of the array while pushing thrust an element into an array. The only problem with the popping method is that you can only remove an element from the end of the array. See the following example to understand how you can do that.

```
<!DOCTYPE html>
<html>
<body>

<p>Learning JavaScript Arrays</p>

<p id="popping-demo1"></p>
<p id="popping-demo2"></p>

<script>
var veggies = ["Pumpkin", "Ginger",
"Tomato", "Garlic"];
document.getElementById("popping-
demo1").innerHTML = veggies;
veggies.pop();
document.getElementById("popping-
demo2").innerHTML = veggies;
</script>

</body>
</html>
```

Learning JavaScript Arrays

```
Pumpkin, Ginger, Tomato, Garlic
Pumpkin, Ginger, Tomato
```

The last item of the array was popped out with the help of the pop() method. You can keep repeating the script, and you will end up with an empty array.

Now you have learned how to pop items from arrays, I will explain how to push elements in. Please remember that you will not see the added element right after running the code. As I have added a button to the code, you will have to click on the button first and then display the element. As the code has a function, the push method will add many instances of the same element to the code. Keeping clicking, and the browser will keep adding more instances to the array.

```html
<!DOCTYPE html>
<html>
<body>

<p>Learning Array Methods</p>

<p>The JavaScript push() method will append
a new element to your arrays.</p>

<button onclick="FunctionYY()">Click
Me</button>

<p id="array-demo"></p>

<script>
```

```
var veggies = ["Garlic", "Pumpkin",
"Ginger", "Tomato"];
document.getElementById("array-
demo").innerHTML = veggies;

function FunctionYY() {
  veggies.push("Spinach");
  document.getElementById("array-
demo").innerHTML = veggies;
}
</script>

</body>
</html>
```

Learning Array Methods

The JavaScript push() method will append a new element to your arrays.

Click Me

Garlic, Pumpkin, Ginger, Tomato, Spinach

Shifting Arrays

There is another method known as the shift method for removing elements from the arrays' starting point. Let us suppose you have got an array. I will use the same veggies array to explain the concept of shifting in arrays. Contrary to the popping method, the shifting method will remove the first element from the array. While the shift method removes one element from the array, the unshift method removes one or more from the beginning of the array.

With the removal of elements, there is a change in the index numbers as well. All the other elements in the array will be automatically shifted to lower indices after you use the shift or unshift method. Once again, merely running the code in the browser will not remove the element from the start. You will have to hit the click me button to trigger the change in the array. Also, if you keep clicking the button, and the browser will keep removing the elements from the array. This is how it will go on end. The shift() method is highly flexible in the sense that you can get the removed elements collected inside a variable. You can then use them at your will and need.

```html
<!DOCTYPE html>
<html>
<body>

<p>Learning Array Methods</p>

<p>The shift()</p>

<button onclick="FunctionYY()">Click Me</button>

<p id="array-demo"></p>

<script>
var veggies = ["Garlic", "Pumpkin", "Ginger", "Tomato"];
document.getElementById("array-demo").innerHTML = veggies;

function FunctionYY() {
  veggies.shift();
```

```
    document.getElementById("array-
demo").innerHTML = veggies;
}
</script>

</body>
</html>
```

Learning Array Methods

The shift()

Click Me

Pumpkin, Ginger, Tomato

There is a method to delete elements from an array. The keyword for the script is labeled as delete.

```
<!DOCTYPE html>
<html>
<body>

<p>Learning Array Methods</p>

<p>The delete method</p>


<p id="array-demo1"></p>
<p id="array-demo2"></p>

<script>
var veggies = ["Garlic ", "Pumpkin ",
"Ginger ", "Tomato "];
```

```
document.getElementById("array-
demo1").innerHTML =
"Here is the first vegetable name " +
veggies[0];
delete veggies[0];
document.getElementById("array-
demo2").innerHTML =
"Here is the first vegetable name: " +
veggies[0];

</script>

</body>
</html>
```

Learning Array Methods

The delete method

Here is the first vegetable name Garlic

Here is the first vegetable name: undefined

The splice() Method

There is a splice() method in JavaScript to add more or multiple elements in the array. The method also removes elements that are placed after it. I will use the same array that I used for the other methods so that you can understand the difference among the methods. The first digit in parentheses is the starting index for the addition or deletion. The second element shows the remaining elements to remove. You can use the splice method for copying consecutive elements at any position you want and then adding them to a new array.

```
<!DOCTYPE html>
<html>
<body>

<p>JavaScript splice()</p>

<p>I will use the splice() method to add new
elements.</p>

<button onclick="FunctionZZ()">Click
Me</button>

<p id="array-demo1"></p>
<p id="array-demo2"></p>

<script>
var veggies = ["Pumpkin ", "Ginger ",
"Tomato ", "Potato "];
document.getElementById("array-
demo1").innerHTML = "You are seeing the
original Array:<br>" + veggies;
function FunctionZZ() {
  veggies.splice(3, 0, "Spinach ", "Garlic
");
  document.getElementById("array-
demo2").innerHTML = "You are seeing the new
Array:<br>" + veggies;
}
</script>

</body>
</html>
```

JavaScript splice()

I will use the splice() method to add new elements.

Click Me

You are seeing the original Array:

Pumpkin, Ginger, Tomato, Potato

You are seeing the new Array:

Pumpkin, Ginger, Tomato, Spinach, Garlic, Potato

If you analyze the code snippet, you will see that there are two parameters in the code. The first parameter (3) points out the position where I instructed the editor to add a new element – in other words, the element was spliced in. The second parameter (0) defined the number of elements that I wanted to remove from the code. The next two parameters instructed the editor to add new elements to the array.

You also can use the splice() method to expel certain elements from the array. Although there are many other methods for the task, the splice() method gives programmers the right way to do away with holes in the array.

```
<!DOCTYPE html>
<html>
<body>

<p>JavaScript splice()</p>

<p>I will use the splice() method to add new
elements.</p>
```

```
<button onclick="FunctionZZ()">Click
Me</button>

<p id="array-demo1"></p>
<p id="array-demo2"></p>

<script>
var veggies = ["Pumpkin ", "Ginger ",
"Tomato ", "Potato "];
document.getElementById("array-
demo1").innerHTML = "You are seeing the
original Array:<br>" + veggies;
function FunctionZZ() {
  veggies.splice(0, 2);
  document.getElementById("array-
demo2").innerHTML = "You are seeing the new
Array:<br>" + veggies;
}
</script>

</body>
</html>
```

JavaScript splice()

I will use the splice() method to add new elements.

Click Me

You are seeing the original Array:

Pumpkin, Ginger, Tomato, Potato

You are seeing the new Array:

Tomato, Potato

In the above-mentioned code snippet, the first parameter (0) defines the point that should be used as a reference for the addition of new elements. The second parameter (1) is used to define the number of elements that must be removed. As I have excluded the previous two additional elements, there will be no addition of new elements.

Concatenation

JavaScript allows you to concatenate two arrays to produce a new array.

```
<!DOCTYPE html>
<html>
<body>

<p>JavaScript Array concat()</p>

<p>The concat() method follows the merging
pattern:</p>

<p id="array-demo"></p>

<script>
var veggies = ["Tomato ", "Potato ",
"Cauliflower ", "Cabbage "];
var frutoos = ["Orange ", "Fig ", "Guava ",
"Date "];
var fruitbasket = veggies.concat(frutoos);

document.getElementById("array-
demo").innerHTML = fruitbasket;
</script>

</body>
</html>
```

JavaScript Array concat()

The concat() method follows the merging pattern:

Tomato, Potato, Cauliflower, Cabbage, Orange, Fig, Guava, Date

The concat() method in JavaScript can be treated with more than two arguments. You can add another array to merge it up with the two. The following example will explain the method by which you can merge up to three arrays.

```
<!DOCTYPE html>
<html>
<body>

<p>JavaScript Array concat()</p>

<p>The concat() method follows the merging
pattern:</p>

<p id="array-demo"></p>

<script>
var veggies = ["Tomato ", "Potato ",
"Cauliflower ", "Cabbage "];
var frutoos = ["Orange ", "Fig ", "Guava ",
"Date "];
var summerfrutoos = ["Watermelon ", "Melon
", "Mango "]
var fruitbasket = veggies.concat(frutoos,
summerfrutoos);

document.getElementById("array-
demo").innerHTML = fruitbasket;
</script>
```

```
</body>
</html>
```

JavaScript Array concat()

The concat() method follows the merging pattern:

Tomato ,Potato ,Cauliflower ,Cabbage ,Orange ,Fig ,Guava ,Date ,Watermelon ,Melon ,Mango

The concat() method also takes strings as arguments. Here is the sample to learn how to add strings to an array.

```
<!DOCTYPE html>
<html>
<body>

<p>JavaScript Array concat()</p>

<p>The concat() method follows the merging
pattern:</p>

<p id="array-demo"></p>

<script>
var veggies = ["Tomato ", "Potato ",
"Cauliflower ", "Cabbage "];
var fruitbasket = veggies.concat('Spinach ',
'garlic ', 'eggplant ');

document.getElementById("array-
demo").innerHTML = fruitbasket;
</script>
```

```
</body>
</html>
```

JavaScript Array concat()

The concat() method follows the merging pattern:

Tomato ,Potato ,Cauliflower ,Cabbage ,Spinach ,garlic ,eggplant

Slicing

You can slice off an array at the point you want. The slice() method produces pieces of the array and creates new arrays.

```
<!DOCTYPE html>
<html>
<body>

<p>JavaScript Array concat()</p>

<p>The concat() method follows the merging pattern:</p>

<p id="array-demo"></p>

<script>
var veggies = ["Tomato ", "Potato ",
"Cauliflower ", "Cabbage "];
var freshveggies = veggies.slice(1);
var freshveggies1 = veggies.slice(2);
document.getElementById("array-
demo").innerHTML = veggies + "<br><br>" +
freshveggies + "<br><br>" + freshveggies1;

</script>
```

```
</body>
</html>
```

JavaScript Array concat()

The concat() method follows the merging pattern:

Tomato ,Potato ,Cauliflower ,Cabbage

Potato ,Cauliflower ,Cabbage

Cauliflower ,Cabbage

The slice() method keeps the existing array intact. It does not delete any new element from the source of the array. The example

```
<!DOCTYPE html>
<html>
<body>

<p>JavaScript Array</p>

<p>The concat() method follows the merging
pattern:</p>

<p id="array-demo"></p>

<script>
var veggies = ["Tomato ", "Potato ",
"Cauliflower ", "Cabbage "];
var freshveggies = veggies.slice(1, 3);
document.getElementById("array-
demo").innerHTML = veggies + "<br><br>" +
freshveggies;
</script>
```

```
</body>
</html>
```

JavaScript Array

The concat() method follows the merging pattern:

Tomato ,Potato ,Cauliflower ,Cabbage

Potato ,Cauliflower

If you omit the ending argument, the result has the entire left out array.

```
<!DOCTYPE html>
<html>
<body>

<p>JavaScript Array</p>

<p>The concat() method follows the merging
pattern:</p>

<p id="array-demo"></p>

<script>
var veggies = ["Tomato ", "Potato ",
"Cauliflower ", "Cabbage "];
var freshveggies = veggies.slice(1);
document.getElementById("array-
demo").innerHTML = veggies + "<br><br>" +
freshveggies;
</script>
```

```
</body>
</html>
```

JavaScript Array

The concat() method follows the merging pattern:

Tomato ,Potato ,Cauliflower ,Cabbage

Potato ,Cauliflower ,Cabbage

Array Sorting

You can use the sort() method to sort out an array in alphabetical order. This is helpful when you are working with a huge number of array items in a retail outlet or a financial firm.

```
<!DOCTYPE html>
<html>
<body>

<p>This is JavaScript Array Sort method</p>

<p>This method will sort out an array in
alphabetical order.</p>

<button onclick="FunctionAlpha()">Please
Click Me</button>

<p id="demo10"></p>

<script>
var veggies = ["Garlic ", "Spinach ",
"Radish ", "Peas ", "Potato "];
```

```
document.getElementById("demo").innerHTML =
veggies;

function FunctionAlpha() {
  veggies.sort();

document.getElementById("demo10").innerHTML
= veggies;
}
</script>

</body>
</html>
```

This is JavaScript Array Sort method

This method will sort out an array in alphabetical order.

Please Click Me

Garlic ,Peas ,Potato ,Radish ,Spinach

Reverse Gear

You can set an array to the reverse position by using the reverse() method. It will put the elements in reverse order. This method is also known as the descending method because it reverses the alphabetical order and sets them into a descending position.

```
<!DOCTYPE html>
<html>
<body>

<p>This is JavaScript Array Sort method</p>
```

```
<p>This method will sort out an array in
alphabetical order.</p>

<button onclick="FunctionAlpha()">Please
Click Me</button>

<p id="demo10"></p>

<script>
var veggies = ["Garlic ", "Spinach ",
"Radish ", "Peas ", "Potato "];
document.getElementById("demo").innerHTML =
veggies;

function FunctionAlpha() {
  veggies.sort();
  veggies.reverse();

document.getElementById("demo10").innerHTML
= veggies;
}
</script>

</body>
</html>
```

This is JavaScript Array Sort method

This method will sort out an array in alphabetical order.

Please Click Me

Spinach ,Radish ,Potato ,Peas ,Garlic

Sorting Numeric

The sort() function is by default tuned to sort the values that are in the form of strings. They work well when you have words to sort out. However, if you have numbers to sort out, you will land in a problematic situation. The number 20 is bigger in the eyes of the sorted function as compared with the number 100. The reason is that 2 is bigger than 1. That's why it is highly likely that you may get incorrect results if you try to apply the sorted() method to arrays.

```
<!DOCTYPE html>
<html>
<body>

<p>Learning JavaScript Array Sort</p>

<p>By clicking the button, you can sort the
array in ascending order.</p>

<button onclick="FunctionT()">Click
Me</button>

<p id="demo10"></p>

<script>
var nums = [4000, 1000, 15, 555, 253, 102];
document.getElementById("demo10").innerHTML
= nums;

function FunctionT() {
  nums.sort(function(x, y){return x - y});

document.getElementById("demo10").innerHTML
= nums;
```

```
}
</script>

</body>
</html>
```

Learning JavaScript Array Sort

By clicking the button, you can sort the array in ascending order.

Click Me

```
4000,1000,15,555,253,102
```

This is how the results look when you run the code in a browser. Now I will hit the button to get the sorted out results. See the difference below.

Learning JavaScript Array Sort

By clicking the button, you can sort the array in ascending order.

Click Me

```
15,102,253,555,1000,4000
```

Now I will use the same sort() method to reverse the order in a descending pattern. Let us see what type of results we can have by this. I will show the results that I get after I click the button on the browser screen.

```
<!DOCTYPE html>
<html>
<body>
```

```
<p>Learning JavaScript Array Sort</p>

<p>By clicking the button, you can sort the
array in ascending order.</p>

<button onclick="FunctionT()">Click
Me</button>

<p id="demo10"></p>

<script>
var nums = [4000, 1000, 15, 555, 253, 102];
document.getElementById("demo10").innerHTML
= nums;

function FunctionT() {
  nums.sort(function(x, y){return y - x});

document.getElementById("demo10").innerHTML
= nums;
}
</script>

</body>
</html>
```

Learning JavaScript Array Sort

By clicking the button, you can sort the array in ascending order.

Click Me

```
4000,1000,555,253,102,15
```

If you get different results, try to click the button and see the results.

Compare Function

You can use the compare function to get the desired results even when you are dealing with numbers. The purpose of this function is to define a specific alternative to the sort order. This compare function must return a zero, negative, or positive value based on what arguments you use. When you feed the sort() function with a couple of values, it dispatches the values to the compare function. After that, it sorts these values as per the returned values that are either negative, positive, or zero. If you see negative results, you will have x sorted out from y. If you see positive results, you will see y sorted before x. The figure zero suggests no change in the sorting order of the values.

This function compares values in an array. When it compares 20 and 100, it will call the compare function, which will calculate the difference. If the result is negative, it will declare 20 as lower in value than 100. You can use the code snippet to make experiments with alphabetic and numeric sorting.

```
<!DOCTYPE html>
<html>
<body>

<p>Learning JavaScript Array Sort</p>
```

```html
<p>You can use the click buttons to sort out
the arrays either in alphabetical order or
in numerical order.</p>

<button onclick="FunctionP()">Click Me to
Sort Alphabetically</button>
<button onclick="FunctionQ()">Click Me to
Sort Numerically</button>

<p id="demo1"></p>

<script>
var nums = [4045, 1002, 1567, 5234, 251,
100];
document.getElementById("demo1").innerHTML =
nums;

function FunctionP() {
  nums.sort();
  document.getElementById("demo1").innerHTML
= nums;
}
function FunctionQ() {
  nums.sort(function(x, y){return x - y});
  document.getElementById("demo1").innerHTML
= nums;
}
</script>

</body>
</html>
```

Learning JavaScript Array Sort

You can use the click buttons to sort out the arrays either in alphabetical order or in numerical order.

Click Me to Sort Alphabetically Click Me to Sort Numerically

4045,1002,1567,5234,251,100

The above result is the original one that is displayed when you run the code in the browser. Here is what happens when you click the button for alphabetic sorting.

Learning JavaScript Array Sort

You can use the click buttons to sort out the arrays either in alphabetical order or in numerical order.

Click Me to Sort Alphabetically Click Me to Sort Numerically

100,1002,1567,251,4045,5234

See the results when you do numeric sorting.

Learning JavaScript Array Sort

You can use the click buttons to sort out the arrays either in alphabetical order or in numerical order.

Click Me to Sort Alphabetically Click Me to Sort Numerically

100,251,1002,1567,4045,5234

Random Sorting

You can use the random method to sort out arrays randomly. See the example to learn how to add the method to the code and get the desired results. By using the random method, you will have random

120

sorting of the numbers. I cannot show all the sorted results here because I get a different result in the browser each time I click the button. You can use the code and see different results by clicking the button multiple times. See the following example.

```
<!DOCTYPE html>
<html>
<body>

<p>Learning JavaScript Array Sort</p>

<p>By clicking the button, you can sort the
array in ascending order.</p>

<button onclick="FunctionT()">Click
Me</button>

<p id="demo10"></p>

<script>
var nums = [4000, 1000, 15, 555, 253, 102];
document.getElementById("demo10").innerHTML
= nums;

function FunctionT() {
  nums.sort(function(x, y){return 0.5 -
Math.random()});

document.getElementById("demo10").innerHTML
= nums;
}
</script>

</body>
</html>
```

Learning JavaScript Array Sort

By clicking the button, you can sort the array in ascending order.

Click Me

15,253,1000,555,102,4000

The problem with the random method is that it favors some numbers over others. There is another method that is more correct and useful than this one. It is commonly known as the Fisher-Yates shuffle. The method was introduced in data science in the early days of data science.

```
<!DOCTYPE html>
<html>
<body>

<p>JavaScript Array Sort Goes On</p>

<h3>This is Fisher-Yates Method</h3>

<p>When you click the button repeatedly, you
will sort the array in random order.</p>

<button onclick="FunctionXX()">Click
Me</button>

<p id="demo12"></p>

<script>
var nums = [404, 10023, 123, 589, 2511,
102];
document.getElementById("demo12").innerHTML
= nums;
```

```
function FunctionXX() {
var a, b, c;
  for (a = nums.length -1; a > 0; a--) {
    b = Math.floor(Math.random() * a)
    c = nums[a]
    nums[a] = nums[b]
    nums[b] = c
  }

document.getElementById("demo12").innerHTML
= nums;
}
</script>

</body>
</html>
```

JavaScript Array Sort Goes On

This is Fisher-Yates Method

When you click the button repeatedly, you will sort the array in random order.

Click Me

```
404,10023,123,589,2511,102
```

Array Values

JavaScript does not have any built-in functions to find out the highest or the lowest value in arrays. However, when you have stored one array, you may use the index for getting the highest and the lowest values.

```
<!DOCTYPE html>
<html>
<body>

<p>JavaScript Array Sorting Method</p>

<p>You are seeing the lowest number which is
<span id="demo4"></span>.</p>

<script>
var nums = [4099999, 124100, 12, 5444,
2544444, 102343];
nums.sort(function(x, y){return x-y});
document.getElementById("demo4").innerHTML =
nums[0];
</script>

</body>
</html>
```

JavaScript Array Sorting Method

You are seeing the lowest number which is 12.

The same code can be used to fish out the highest number. I will reverse the pattern and hunt down the highest number in the list. Here is the pattern.

```
<!DOCTYPE html>
<html>
<body>

<p>JavaScript Array Sorting Method</p>
```

```
<p>You are seeing the lowest number which is
<span id="demo4"></span>.</p>

<script>
var nums = [4099999, 124100, 12, 5444,
2544444, 102343];
nums.sort(function(x, y){return y - x});
document.getElementById("demo4").innerHTML =
nums[0];
</script>

</body>
</html>
```

JavaScript Array Sorting Method

You are seeing the lowest number which is 4099999.

This method to find out the highest and the lowest values in an array is the dumbest method. It also is inefficient as well. If you want to be more precise and accurate, you can use the Math.max() method and reach the most accurate number without sifting through an entire array and returning the answer afterward.

```
<!DOCTYPE html>
<html>
<body>

<p>JavaScript Array Sorting through Max
method</p>

<p>Here is the highest number in the array:
<span id="demo7"></span>.</p>

<script>
```

```
var nums = [4087787878, 1002333333333, 112,
5, 2544, 11220];
document.getElementById("demo7").innerHTML =
ArrayMaxPoint(nums);

function ArrayMaxPoint(arr) {
  return Math.max.apply(null, arr);
}
</script>

</body>
</html>
```

JavaScript Array Sorting through Max Method

Here is the highest number in the array: 1002333333333.

Now I will use the same method to find out the lowest value in the array. See the following example.

```
<!DOCTYPE html>
<html>
<body>

<p>JavaScript Array Sorting through Max
method</p>

<p>Here is the highest number in the array:
<span id="demo7"></span>.</p>

<script>
var nums = [4087787878, 1002333333333, 112,
5, 2544, 11220];
document.getElementById("demo7").innerHTML =
ArrayMaxPoint(nums);
```

```
function ArrayMaxPoint(arr) {
  return Math.min.apply(null, arr);
}
</script>

</body>
</html>
```

JavaScript Array Sorting through Max Method

Here is the highest number in the array: 5.

Here is another solution that is considered the fastest way to detect the highest numbers in an array. In this method, a function enters a loop and iterates through the array to compare every single value of the array with the top value that it detects at the first stage. When it has looped through all the values, it produces the result.

```
<!DOCTYPE html>
<html>
<body>

<p>JavaScript Array Sorting for highest
value</p>

<p>Here is the highest number in the array:
<span id="demo7"></span>.</p>

<script>
var nums = [4077879878, 10023, 147777777777,
53, 25, 1023];
document.getElementById("demo7").innerHTML =
ArrayMaxPoint(nums);

function ArrayMaxPoint(arr) {
```

```
    var length = arr.length;
    var maximum = -Infinity;
    while (length--) {
      if (arr[length] > maximum) {
        maximum = arr[length];
      }
    }
    return maximum;
}
</script>

</body>
</html>
```

JavaScript Array Sorting for Highest Value

Here is the highest number in the array: 147777777777.

Similarly, you can create a function that will loop through the entire array to detect first the lowest value and then compare it with the rest of the values of the array. Finally, it will produce the result in the browser. See how the minimum function works and loops through the array.

```
<!DOCTYPE html>
<html>
<body>

<p>JavaScript Array Sorting for highest
value</p>

<p>Here is the highest number in the array:
<span id="demo7"></span>.</p>

<script>
```

```
var nums = [4077879878, 10023, 147777777777,
53, 25, 1023];
document.getElementById("demo7").innerHTML =
ArrayMinPoint(nums);

function ArrayMinPoint(arr) {
  var length = arr.length;
  var minimum = Infinity;
  while (length--) {
    if (arr[length] < minimum) {
      minimum = arr[length];
    }
  }
  return minimum;
}
</script>

</body>
</html>
```

JavaScript Array Sorting for Highest Value

Here is the highest number in the array: 25.

Object Array Sorting

If you have an array with objects, you can sort them with the following method.

```
<!DOCTYPE html>
<html>
<body>

<p>JavaScript Array Sorting Objects</p>
```

129

```
<p>Please click the buttons to sort out the
objects of the car.</p>

<button onclick="FunctionO()">Please Click
Me to Sort</button>

<p id="demo2"></p>

<script>
var carsObjects = [
  {type:"Honda", year:2020, Make:"Japan",
Model:"Vezel"},
  {type:"Toyota", year:2010, Make:"Japan",
Model:"Fortuner"},
  {type:"Toyota", year:2018, Make:"Japan",
Model:"Vitz"}
];

ToDisplayCars();

function FunctionO() {
  carsObjects.sort(function(x, y){return
x.year - y.year});
  ToDisplayCars();
}

function ToDisplayCars() {
  document.getElementById("demo2").innerHTML
=
  carsObjects[0].type + " " +
carsObjects[0].year + " " +
carsObjects[0].Make + " " +
carsObjects[0].Model + "<br>" +
  carsObjects[1].type + " " +
carsObjects[1].year + " " +
```

```
carsObjects[0].Make + " " +
carsObjects[0].Model + "<br>" +
  carsObjects[2].type + " " +
carsObjects[2].year + " " +
carsObjects[0].Make + " " +
carsObjects[0].Model;
}
</script>

</body>
</html>
```

JavaScript Array Sorting Objects

Please click the buttons to sort out the objects of the car.

Please Click Me to Sort

Toyota 2010 Japan Fortuner

Toyota 2018 Japan Fortuner

Honda 2020 Japan Fortuner

I have already sorted it by clicking the sorting button. You may see a different order when you run the code first in the browser. The order will only change when hit the sorting button.

JavaScript Iteration

There is more in JavaScript arrays that you can learn and apply when you are creating web pages. The forEach() method helps you make a function call for all the elements of the array.

```
<!DOCTYPE html>
<html>
<body>

<p>This is JavaScript Array.forEach()</p>

<p>This method makes a function call at
least once for all individual array
elements.</p>

<p id="demo44"></p>

<script>
var msg = "";
var nums = [4588888, 2234, 12349, 16899,
900025];
nums.forEach(FunctionE);
document.getElementById("demo44").innerHTML
= msg;

function FunctionE(Evalue, Eindex, Earray) {
  msg = msg + Evalue + "<br>";
}
</script>

</body>
</html>
```

This is JavaScript Array.forEach()

This method makes a function call at least once for all individual array elements.

4588888

2234

12349

16899

900025

I have allocated three arguments to the function; the first argument deals with the value of the item, the second argument deals with the item's index, and the third argument deals with the array as a whole. I have only deployed the Evalue parameter in the above-mentioned example. This means that if you do not need the other two, you can slice them off of the function to simplify the code. However, If you think you are going to need the other two, you can keep them and use them later on in separate function calls. The best thing about Array.forEach() method is that it suits well to all web browsers except Internet Explorer 8 or its previous versions.

The map() Method

The map() method is used by programmers to create a new array by performing an individual function on all array elements. It does not execute the function for the elements that are void of values, and it does not change the original form of the array. The following example will have an addition operator adding 1000 to each number in the array and creating a new array that way.

```
<!DOCTYPE html>
<html>
<body>

<p>This is JavaScript Array.map()</p>

<p>I will create a new array by applying the
function on all array elements.</p>
```

```
<p id="demo90"></p>

<script>
var nums1 = [12345, 7674, 3449, 12316,
9900025];
var nums2 = nums1.map(FunctionM);

document.getElementById("demo90").innerHTML
= nums2;

function FunctionM(Mvalue, Mindex, Marray) {
   return Mvalue + 1000;
}
</script>

</body>
</html>
```

This is JavaScript Array.map()

I will create a new array by applying the function on all array elements.

```
13345,8674,4449,13316,9901025
```

I will remove the plus operator and add the multiplication operator to produce different results and create a new array.

```
<!DOCTYPE html>
<html>
<body>

<p>This is JavaScript Array.map()</p>

<p>I will create a new array by applying the
function on all array elements.</p>
```

```
<p id="demo90"></p>

<script>
var nums1 = [12345, 7674, 3449, 12316,
9900025];
var nums2 = nums1.map(FunctionM);

document.getElementById("demo90").innerHTML
= nums2;

function FunctionM(Mvalue, Mindex, Marray) {
  return Mvalue * 1000;
}
</script>

</body>
</html>
```

This is JavaScript Array.map()

I will create a new array by applying the function on all array elements.

```
12345000,7674000,3449000,12316000,9900025000
```

Please note that the function that I have included in the code takes three arguments; the first argument is for value, the second is for index, and the third is for the array as a whole. If you need to work with only one parameter, you may omit the rest of the parameters. The omission will not affect the program. It will produce the same results. Just like the preceding method, Array.map() works well on all web browsers except internet explorer 8 or its earlier versions.

The filter() Method

The filter() method tends to create a new array with the elements of the array that manage to pass the test. I will set the filter bar at number 20, which means that all the numbers that are above 20 will be filtered out by the method. Users will only see the numbers that are over 20. The rest of the elements will be hidden.

```html
<!DOCTYPE html>
<html>
<body>

<p>This is JavaScript Array.filter()</p>

<p>The following program will create a new
array by filtering all array elements that
tend to pass the test.</p>

<p id="demo789"></p>

<script>
var nums = [45890, 17, 3459, 18, 2, 6,
23416, 87625];
var over20 = nums.filter(FunctionZ);

document.getElementById("demo789").innerHTML
= over20;

function FunctionZ(valueF, indexF, arrayF) {
  return valueF > 20;
}
</script>

</body>
</html>
```

This is JavaScript Array.filter()

The following program will create a new array by filtering all array elements that tend to pass the test.

```
45890,3459,23416,87625
```

The reduce() Method

The reduce() method makes a function call to all the array elements and produces one value. The method will operate from left to right inside the array. It keeps the original array intact.

```
<!DOCTYPE html>
<html>
<body>

<p>This is JavaScript Array.reduce()</p>

<p>The following program will create a new
array by reducing all array elements that
tend to pass the test.</p>

<p id="demo789"></p>

<script>
var nums = [45890, 17, 3459, 18, 2, 6,
23416, 87625];
var over20 = nums.reduce(FunctionZ);

document.getElementById("demo789").innerHTML
= over20;

function FunctionZ(Total, valueF) {
   return Total + valueF;
}
```

```
</script>

</body>
</html>
```

This is JavaScript Array.reduce()

The following program will create a new array by filtering all array elements that tend to pass the test.

160433

The most amazing thing about the reduce() method is that it takes an additional value to start with unlike other methods.

```
<!DOCTYPE html>
<html>
<body>

<p>This is JavaScript Array.filter()</p>

<p>The following program will create a new
array by filtering all array elements that
tend to pass the test.</p>

<p id="demo789"></p>

<script>
var nums = [45890, 17, 3459, 18, 2, 6,
23416, 87625];
var over20 = nums.reduce(FunctionZ,
5000000000);

document.getElementById("demo789").innerHTML
= over20;
```

```
function FunctionZ(Total, valueF) {
  return Total + valueF;
}
</script>

</body>
</html>
```

This is JavaScript Array.filter()

The following program will create a new array by filtering all array elements that tend to pass the test.

```
5000160433
```

The reduceRight() Method

The reduceRigth() method tends to run a function on all elements of an array to produce one value. This method works well, moving from the right side to the left side of the array. The best thing is that you will be able to keep the original array intact.

```
<!DOCTYPE html>
<html>
<body>

<p>This is JavaScript Array. reduceRight
()</p>

<p>The following program will create a new
array by filtering all array elements that
tend to pass the test.</p>

<p id="demo789"></p>

<script>
```

```
var nums = [45890, 17, 3459, 18, 2, 6,
23416, 87625900000];
var sum = nums.reduceRight(FunctionZ);

document.getElementById("demo789").innerHTML
= "The Total sum of all the numbers is " +
sum;

function FunctionZ(Total, valueF) {
   return Total + valueF;
}
</script>

</body>
</html>
```

This is JavaScript Array.reduceRight()

The following program will create a new array by filtering all array elements that tend to pass the test.

The Total sum of all the numbers is 87625972808

The Array.reduceRigth() works well on all the web browsers except the Internet Explorer 8 or the earlier versions.

The every() Method

The every() method runs a thorough check through the arrays to see if all the elements in the array pass a test. In the following example, I will run a test to see if all the elements are bigger than 500 or not.

```
<!DOCTYPE html>
<html>
<body>
```

```
<p>This is JavaScript Array.every()</p>

<p>The following program will display the
results of the test.</p>

<p id="demo789"></p>

<script>
var nums = [45890, 17, 3459, 18, 2, 6,
23416, 87625900000];
var Over500 = nums.every(FunctionZ);

document.getElementById("demo789").innerHTML
= "Are all values bigger than 500: " +
Over500;

function FunctionZ(valueF) {
   return valueF > 500;
}
</script>

</body>
</html>
```

This is JavaScript Array.every()

The following program will display the results of the test.

Are all values bigger than 500: false

Now I will deliberately make all the values bigger than 500 and what the result is.

```
<!DOCTYPE html>
<html>
<body>
```

```
<p>This is JavaScript Array.every()</p>

<p>The following program will display the
results of the test.</p>

<p id="demo789"></p>

<script>
var nums = [45890, 1700, 3459, 1800, 2700,
6222, 23416, 87625900000];
var Over500 = nums.every(FunctionZ);

document.getElementById("demo789").innerHTML
= "Are all values bigger than 500: " +
Over500;

function FunctionZ(valueF) {
   return valueF > 500;
}
</script>

</body>
</html>
```

This is JavaScript Array.every()

The following program will display the results of the test.

Are all values bigger than 500: true

The some() Method

There is another method that is used to check how many values of an array have passed the test. I will check how many values have passed the over 500 test. The method may take more than one argument but as I need one, I will stick to that. You can add more arguments to sift through the index and produce the entire array.

```
<!DOCTYPE html>
<html>
<body>

<p>This is JavaScript Array.some()</p>

<p>The following program will display the
results of the test.</p>

<p id="demo789"></p>

<script>
var nums = [45890, 170, 345, 1800, 270, 622,
23416, 87625900000];
var Over500 = nums.some(FunctionZ);

document.getElementById("demo789").innerHTML
= "Are there some values bigger than 500: "
+ Over500;

function FunctionZ(valueF) {
  return valueF > 500;
}
</script>

</body>
</html>
```

This is JavaScript Array.some()

The following program will display the results of the test.

Are there some values bigger than 500: true

The indexOf() Method

The indexOf() method combs through the array to search for a value and then return the position of the value. The first item on the list has a position 0 while the second item has a positon 1.

```html
<!DOCTYPE html>
<html>
<body>

<p>This is JavaScript Array.indexOf()</p>

<p>The following program will display the
index of the elements of the array.</p>

<p id="demo789"></p>

<script>
var nums = [45890, 170, 345, 1800, 270, 622,
23416, 87625900000];
var p = nums.indexOf(622);

document.getElementById("demo789").innerHTML
= "The position of 622 in the array is: " +
p;

</script>

</body>
</html>
```

This is JavaScript Array.indexOf()

The following program will display the index of the elements of the array.

The position of 622 in the array is: 5

Let us analyze the syntax of the method. At the start, you need to write the name of the item that the method must search for. The second part is optional. You may tell the code about the starting point of the search. The negative values will start at a specific position and counting will start from the last point. The search will go on to the end. If the browser does not find the item, it will return -1 as a result. If the item has more than one instant presence in the array, it will display the first occurrence's position.

```
<!DOCTYPE html>
<html>
<body>

<p>This is Array.lastIndexOf()</p>

<p id="demo00"></p>

<script>
var veggies = ["Garlic", "Tomatoes",
"Potatoes", "Tomatoes", "Pumpkin",
"Tomatoes"];
var a = veggies.lastIndexOf("Tomatoes");
document.getElementById("demo00").innerHTML
= "Tomatoes are found at position " + (a);
</script>

</body>
</html>
```

This is Array.lastIndexOf()

Tomatoes are found at position 5

The find() Method

The find() method gives you the value of the first item in the array that will pass the test function.

```
<!DOCTYPE html>
<html>
<body>

<p>This is Array.find()</p>


<p id="demo00"></p>

<script>
var nums = [444, 55544, 2333, 56666, 22,
876];
var a = nums.find(FunctionZ);
document.getElementById("demo00").innerHTML
= "The number that is bigger than 500 = " +
a;

function FunctionZ(valueF) {
   return valueF > 500;
}
</script>

</body>
</html>
```

This is Array.find()

The number that is bigger than 500 = 55544

The findIndex() Method

The findIndex() method will return the index number of the first element of your array that will go through and pass a test. As the array we are working on is made of numbers, I will put a condition that the array will test each number to check if it is lesser than 500 or not.

```
<!DOCTYPE html>
<html>
<body>

<p>This is Array.findIndex()</p>


<p id="demo055"></p>

<script>
var nums = [444, 55544, 2333, 56, 22, 876];
var a = nums.findIndex(FunctionZ);
document.getElementById("demo055").innerHTML
= "The index of the number that is lower
than 500 = " + a;

function FunctionZ(valueF) {
   return valueF < 500;
}
</script>

</body>
</html>
```

This is Array.findIndex()

The index of the number that is lower than 500 = 0

Chapter Six

JavaScript Loops

The JavaScript for loop contains a statement and three expressions. There is an initialization part that runs before the first execution on the for loop. This expression is used for the creation of counters. The variables that you create here are immediately scoped into the for loop. Once the loop is executed and reached its logical end, these variables get destroyed.

Another important of the JavaScript for loop is the condition. The for loop checks this expression before the execution of each new iteration. If you omit this part, the expression is evaluated as true, and the statement in the loop is executed. If the evaluation is false, the loop stops working.

Another important part of the loop is final-expression. This expression is run after each iteration. It is used for incrementing the counter. However, you can also use it for decrementing the counter as well. The statement part of the loop is the code that has to repeat inside of the loop. You can omit any of these expressions from the for loop as per need.

For loops in JavaScript are used to count mathematical numbers or iterations of a statement. They can also repeat a statement in the code. You can exit a loop only after you have inserted in it a break statement. I will explore more the break statement in the following sections.

Loops are special because they save from the hassle of writing a code multiple times. It repeats the code once you have included it in the loop. How many times a code block should be repeated depends on the number you include in the code. Also, each time the loop executes the code, the value will be different. So, although there is the repetition of the code, the repetition proceeds with some proper method.

```
<!DOCTYPE html>
<html>
<body>

<p id="forloop-demo"></p>

<script>
var carsforsale = ["Honda", "Toyota",
"Vezel", "Fiat", "Volkswagen"];
var msg = "";
var YY;
for (YY = 0; YY < carsforsale.length; YY++)
{
   msg += carsforsale[YY] + "<br>";
}
document.getElementById("forloop-
demo").innerHTML = msg;
</script>
```

```
</body>
</html>
```

Honda

Toyota

Vezel

Fiat

Volkswagen

In this example, I created an array and then added a for loop to iterate through the elements of the array. The for loop iterated through the items of the array and displayed them neatly on independent lines.

```
<!DOCTYPE html>
<html>
<body>

<p id="demo1"></p>

<script>
var msg = "";
var YY;
for (YY = 0; YY < 3; YY++) {
  msg += "The next number you will have to
add to the list is " + YY + "<br>";
}
document.getElementById("demo1").innerHTML =
msg;
</script>
```

```
</body>
</html>
```

The next number you will have to add to the list is 0

The next number you will have to add to the list is 1

The next number you will have to add to the list is 2

In this example, the first statement sets up a variable even before the initiation of the loop. The second statement defines the proper condition for this loop to run. According to the condition, the loop must not run more than three times. The third statement increases the value of the variable by YY++ each time the for loop executes the code.

Usually, you need to use the first statement to initialize the variable in the loop. However, this must not always happen. JavaScript does not make it mandatory to start with the first statement. You can skip it and initialize different values in the first statement.

```
<!DOCTYPE html>
<html>
<body>

<p id="demo1"></p>

<script>
var carsforsale = ["Vezel", "Fortuner",
"Sportage", "Sorento"];
var YY, length, msg;
for (YY = 0, length = carsforsale.length,
msg = ""; YY < length; YY++) {
```

```
    msg += carsforsale[YY] + "<br>";
  }
document.getElementById("demo1").innerHTML =
msg;
</script>

</body>
</html>
```

Vezel

Fortuner

Sportage

Sorento

You also can skip the first statement as if your values have been set before the initiation of the loop.

```
<!DOCTYPE html>
<html>
<body>

<p id="demo1"></p>

<script>
var carsforsale = ["Vezel", "Fortuner",
"Sportage", "Sorento"];
var YY = 0
var length = carsforsale.length
var msg = ""
for (; YY < length; YY++) {
  msg += carsforsale[YY] + "<br>";
}
```

```
document.getElementById("demo1").innerHTML =
msg;
</script>

</body>
</html>
```

Vezel

Fortuner

Sportage

Sorento

The second statement in the for loop is often used to evaluate the condition of the starting variable. However, this may not be the case always. JavaScript does not care anymore. The second statement is optional. If the second statement returns as true, the loop will restart all over again. If it returns otherwise, the loop is going to end. If there is an omission of the second statement, you ought to insert a break into the loop. Otherwise, the loop will be infinite. You will never be able to stop it. An infinite loop is a dead-end for you because when a user opens your website that contains an infinite loop, his or her browser will crash. The user will be unlikely to return to your website.

The third statement increments the value of the starting variable. However, the third statement is optional. It can do things like negative incrementing, positive incrementing, and much more. You can omit the third statement as well.

```
<!DOCTYPE html>
<html>
<body>

<p id="demo1"></p>

<script>
var carsforsale = ["Vezel", "Fortuner",
"Sportage", "Sorento"];

var YY = 0
var length = carsforsale.length
var msg = ""

for (; YY < length; YY++) {
  msg += carsforsale[YY] + "<br>";
  YY++;
}
document.getElementById("demo1").innerHTML =
msg;
</script>

</body>
</html>
```

Vezel

Sportage

The most important things to keep in mind are that the counter YY serves important purposes. It keeps in its memory the number of iterations so that it can halt looping at the exact point. It also serves as the index number of an array, allowing the code to move through the array elements as the counter progresses and increments with the iterations.

The variable name YY cannot be considered as sacred. The name can be different. You can choose one according to your liking as long as the name is legal and it corresponds to the naming rules. Most programmers also use i as a variable because it indicates the number of iterations that the program must perform.

The for/in Loop

Another type of the for loop is JavaScript for/in loop. This loop iterates through all the properties of a particular object.

```
<!DOCTYPE html>
<html>
<body>

<p>Learning JavaScript For/In Loop</p>

<p>Our for/in loops through all the
properties of the object car.</p>

<p id="demo1"></p>

<script>
var msg = "";
var car = {name:"Honda", model:"Vezel",
year:2020, make:"Japan"};
var YY;
for (YY in car) {
  msg += car[YY] + " ";
}
document.getElementById("demo1").innerHTML =
msg;
</script>

</body>
```

```
</html>
```

Learning JavaScript For/In Loop

Our for/in loops through all the properties of the object car.

Honda Vezel 2020 Japan

In this example, the for in loop tends to iterate through the object car. With each iteration it returns the key (YY). The program uses the key to access a specific value of the key that is car[YY].

The for/in loop is special because you can pair it up with an array and it will loop through the properties of the array just like it did with the properties of the object.

```
<!DOCTYPE html>
<html>

<head>
<meta content="text/html; charset=windows-
1050" http-equiv="Cont-Type">
</head>

<body>

<p>These are JavaScript For In Loops</p>

<p>I will show how the for/in statement loop
through and over Array values.</p>

<p id="demo5"></p>

<script>
var msg = "";
```

```
var nums = [5545, 24, 139, 6716, 4425];
var YY;
for (YY in nums) {
   msg += nums[YY] + "<br>";
}
document.getElementById("demo5").innerHTML =
msg;
</script>

</body>
</html>
```

These are JavaScript For In Loops

I will show how the for/in statement loop through and over Array values.

5545

24

139

6716

4425

You should drop the idea of using for in over the array loops if you are keen on the order of the index. The order is independent of implementation. You cannot access values of the array in the order that you expect. It is important and better for you to use a for of loop, for loop, and the Array.forEach() whenever you think the order is special.

The forEach() Loop

This method calls a function, also known as the callback function, one time for each element of the array.

```
<!DOCTYPE html>
<html>
<body>

<p>Learning JavaScript Array.forEach()
loops</p>

<p>This program will call a function one
time for each element of the array.</p>

<p id="demo5"></p>

<script>
var msg = "";
var nums = [55545, 454, 1239, 78816, 45625];
nums.forEach(FunctionYZ);
document.getElementById("demo5").innerHTML =
msg;

function FunctionYZ(fvalue, findex, farray)
{
  msg = msg + fvalue + "<br>";
}
</script>

</body>
</html>
```

Learning JavaScript Array.forEach() loops

This program will call a function one time for each element of the array.

55545

454

1239

78816

45625

The function in the above-mentioned code usually takes in three arguments. The first argument is the value of the item. The second argument is the index of the item, and the third argument is the array itself. As the example uses only the value parameter, you can rewrite it in the following pattern.

```
<!DOCTYPE html>
<html>
<body>

<p>Learning JavaScript Array.forEach()
loops</p>

<p>This program will call a function one
time for each element of the array.</p>

<p id="demo5"></p>

<script>
var msg = "";
var nums = [55545, 454, 1239, 78816, 45625];
nums.forEach(FunctionYZ);
document.getElementById("demo5").innerHTML =
msg;
```

```
function FunctionYZ(fvalue) {
  msg = msg + fvalue + "<br>";
}
</script>

</body>
</html>
```

Learning JavaScript Array.forEach() loops

This program will call a function one time for each element of the array.

55545

454

1239

78816

45625

I have excluded all the other parameters except fvalue and still got the same result.

The for/of Loop

There is another type of for loops in JavaScript, known as the for/of statement. This statement loops through the values of a particular object that can be iterated. This statement allows you to create a loop through all kinds of data structures like Maps, Arrays, NodeLists, and Strings.

When an iteration starts, the value of the next property is automatically assigned to a variable. Variables in JavaScript are declared with var, const and let keywords. We have already covered all the topics in the past chapters.

Safari 7, Chrome 38, Opera 25, Edge 12, and Firefox 51 are the only browsers that presently support the for/of statements. Internet Explorer does not support it.

```
<!DOCTYPE html>
<html>
<body>

<p>These are JavaScript For/Of Loop</p>

<p>The for/of statement will create a loop
through all the values of objects that you
can iterate through.</p>

<p id="demo6"></p>

<script>
let carsforsale = ["Volkswagen", "Vezel",
"Ford", "Fortuner", "Sportage"];
let msg = "";

for (let YY of carsforsale) {
  msg += YY + "<br>";
}

document.getElementById("demo6").innerHTML =
msg;
</script>

</body>
```

```
</html>
```

These are JavaScript For/Of Loop

The for/of statement will create a loop through all the values of objects that you can iterate through.

Volkswagen

Vezel

Ford

Fortuner

Sportage

In the next example, I will use a string instead of an array to get the same result.

```
<!DOCTYPE html>
<html>
<body>

<p>These are JavaScript For/Of Loop</p>

<p>The for/of statement will create a loop
through all the values of objects that you
can iterate through.</p>

<p id="demo6"></p>

<script>
let carsforsale = "Volkswagen, Vezel, Ford";
let msg = "";
```

```
for (let YY of carsforsale) {
  msg += YY + "<br>";
}

document.getElementById("demo6").innerHTML =
msg;
</script>

</body>
</html>
```

These are JavaScript For/Of Loop

The for/of statement will create a loop through all the values of objects that you can iterate through.

V
o
l
k
s
w
a
g
e
n
,

V
e
z

163

e

l

,

F

o

r

d

Eternal Loops

When you create a loop, and it doesn't have an ending point, it is called an eternal loop. A loop keeps on going until the computer or browser crashes in a condition. Eternal loops may happen by accident or by blatant carelessness. Eternal loops are bad, and they have the tendency to slow down the web page, driving away the visitors. You may create an eternal loop if you fail to insert a condition in the code that makes the loop to stop after completing the intended iterations.

JavaScript while Loops

JavaScript loops execute codes as long as specific conditions stay true. Now that you have learned about the for loops, I will go on to explain how the while loops work. The while loops iterate as long as certain conditions stay true.

I will create an example in which the while loop runs as long as the condition stands true.

```
<!DOCTYPE html>
```

```
<html>
<body>

<p>Learning JavaScript While Loops</p>

<p id="demo7"></p>

<script>
var msg = "";
var YY = 0;
while (YY < 10) {
  msg += "<br>The next digit is " + YY;
  YY++;
}
document.getElementById("demo7").innerHTML =
msg;
</script>

</body>
</html>
```

Learning JavaScript While Loops

The	next	digit	is	0
The	next	digit	is	1
The	next	digit	is	2
The	next	digit	is	3
The	next	digit	is	4

The next digit is 5

The do/while Loop

The do/while loop is considered a variant of the while loop. It will execute the code once before testing the condition. After that, the loop will be repeated as long as the specific condition is true. One thing that distinguishes the do/while from other loops is that it executes the code once, even if you have set the condition to false. This happens because the browser executes the code even before testing the condition.

```
<!DOCTYPE html>
<html>
<body>

<p>This is JavaScript Do/While Loop</p>

<p id="demo8"></p>

<script>
var msg = ""
var YY = 0;

do {
  msg += "<br>The next digit is " + YY;
  YY++;
}
while (YY < 5);

document.getElementById("demo8").innerHTML =
msg;
</script>

</body>
</html>
```

166

This is JavaScript Do/While Loop

The next digit is 0

The next digit is 1

The next digit is 2

The next digit is 3

The next digit is 4

If you analyze and run a comparison between the for and while loops, you will realize that the two loops are almost the same. The while loop is very much the same as the for loop. However, the only difference is that the first and the third statements are omitted here. I will use the same example and test the for and while loops on it to see how much difference exists between the two. In the first part, I will use the for loop.

```
<!DOCTYPE html>
<html>
<body>

<p id="demo9"></p>

<script>
var carsforsale = ["Vezel", "Fortuner",
"Land Cruiser", "Jimmy"];
var YY = 0;
var msg = "";
for (;carsforsale[YY];) {
  msg += carsforsale[YY] + "<br>";
  YY++;
```

```
}
document.getElementById("demo9").innerHTML =
msg;
</script>

</body>
</html>
```

Vezel

Fortuner

Land Cruiser

Jimmy

In the following, I will use the while loop to collect the names of the cars for sale and then display them neatly in the browser.

```
<!DOCTYPE html>
<html>
<body>

<p id="demo9"></p>

<script>
var carsforsale = ["Vezel", "Fortuner",
"Land Cruiser", "Jimmy"];
var YY = 0;
var msg = "";
while (carsforsale[YY]) {
  msg += carsforsale[YY] + "<br>";
  YY++;
}
```

```
document.getElementById("demo9").innerHTML =
msg;
</script>

</body>
</html>
```

Vezel

Fortuner

Land Cruiser

Jimmy

JavaScript Break and Continue Statements

The break and continue statements are inherently related to for and while loops. The break statement allows you to jump out of the loop and the continue statement to make a jump over one specific iteration inside the loop. The later statement does not break the loop. The program continues to move on. I have already explained the break statement when I discussed the switch statement in the previous chapters. However, there its use was different as it was applied to the switch statements. Now I will use the break statement in the loops.

```
<!DOCTYPE html>
<html>
<body>

<p>Learning JavaScript Loops</p>
```

```
<p>I will integrate a <b>break</b> statement
to the for loop.</p>

<p id="demo9"></p>

<script>
var msg = "";
var YY;
for (YY = 0; YY < 10; YY++) {
   if (YY === 5) { break; }
   msg += "The next digit is " + YY + "<br>";
}
document.getElementById("demo9").innerHTML =
msg;
</script>

</body>
</html>
```

Learning JavaScript Loops

I will integrate a **break** statement to the for loop.

The	next	digit	is	0
The	next	digit	is	1
The	next	digit	is	2
The	next	digit	is	3

The next digit is 4

The loop had to complete the iteration through 10 digits, but as I added a break statement at position 5, the loop broke out of iterations, and the program stopped. The continue statement cannot be said to be the opposite of the break statement because, like the break statement, it also breaks the loop but then continues with the rest of the iterations of the program. I will use the same example to elaborate upon how you can benefit from the continue statement.

```
<!DOCTYPE html>
<html>
<body>

<p>Learning JavaScript Loops</p>

<p>I will integrate a <b>break</b> statement
to the for loop.</p>

<p id="demo9"></p>

<script>
var msg = "";
var YY;
for (YY = 0; YY < 10; YY++) {
  if (YY === 5) { continue; }
  msg += "The next digit is " + YY + "<br>";
}
document.getElementById("demo9").innerHTML =
msg;
</script>

</body>
</html>
```

Learning JavaScript Loops

I will integrate a **break** statement to the for loop.

The next digit is 0

The next digit is 1

The next digit is 2

The next digit is 3

The next digit is 4

The next digit is 6

The next digit is 7

The next digit is 8

The next digit is 9

The loop broke at point 5 and then continued. You can see that the only number that is missing in the results is number 5. The continue statement is suitable for skipping one iteration of a loop. The break statement has only one purpose: to give you a jump out of a switch or a loop. You can use the break statement to make a jump out of a code block.

Chapter Seven

JavaScript Functions

U ntil now, we have created scripts that run the minute the web page loads up in a browser. There is another way to use the code. You can pack up the code inside a function and run it in the web browser. Unless you make a function call, you will not see anything in action on the browser. A function phrase contains the function keyword, the name of the function, and curly braces.

You have to include a space after the function keyword. After that, you need to write the name that you choose to give to your function. These are quite similar to the variable-name tradition. However, the only difference in the naming of functions is that you can add a number, a letter, $ 0r underscores to the name of a function. After this, you need to add a set of round brackets or parentheses to include any arguments. After that, you need to put in the curly brackets to write the code. You don't have to write your function on multiple lines. You can write it on a single line if you are comfortable with that. However, it is better to write it on multiple lines at the start so that you get a clear idea of how it is written. In addition, you can correct any mistake easily if the code does not work well.

A JavaScript function is created to perform a special task. You can execute it when you make a function call.

```
<!DOCTYPE html>
<html>
<body>

<p>Learning JavaScript Functions</p>

<p>In this example I will make a function
call to perform a calculation and gives back
the result:</p>

<p id="demo890"></p>

<script>
function FunctionZZ(x1, x2) {
   return x1 * x2;
}
document.getElementById("demo890").innerHTML
= FunctionZZ(345, 1222);
</script>

</body>
</html>
```

Learning JavaScript Functions

In this example, I will make a function call to perform a calculation and gives back the result:

```
421590
```

You can see that there is a function keyword that is followed by the name of the function. I have included the parentheses in the code. You may include one or more parameters in the parentheses. The code that you need to include in the function is put inside the curly brackets. As for the function arguments, you have to pass them when you have created a function, and now you want to invoke it. Inside of it, the arguments tend to behave very much like local variables. A function works the same way as a Subroutine, and a Procedure do in other programming languages.

The Invocation of Function

The code that you pack up inside a function will only execute if and when you invoke the function. The process of invoking is also called making a function call. It may happen when a visitor hits a button on a web page, or you can invoke it from the JavaScript code. You may also set the function on self-invoked.

There is a return at the end of a function. When you reach it, the function will cease to execute. Functions more often compute the return value, and the value is then returned to the one who made the function call.

```
<!DOCTYPE html>
<html>
<body>

<p>Learning JavaScript Functions</p>
```

```
<p>In this example I will make a function
call to perform a calculation and gives back
the result:</p>

<p id="demo890"></p>

<script>
var Y = FunctionZZ(55, 2345)
document.getElementById("demo890").innerHTML
= Y;

function FunctionZZ(x1, x2) {
   return x1 * x2;
}
</script>

</body>
</html>
```

Learning JavaScript Functions

In this example I will make a function call to perform a calculation and gives back the result:

```
128975
```

In the following example, you will see how I will reuse the code many times after creating it once. You can fill it up with as many arguments as you like and produce different results. This saves time and effort when you are developing a web page. This also makes the process of coding faster and efficient. See the following example.

```
<!DOCTYPE html>
```

```
<html>
<body>

<p>This will make a function call to convert
digits from Fahrenheit to Celsius:</p>
<p id="demo789"></p>

<script>
function toCels(f) {
  return (15/90) * (f-40);
}
document.getElementById("demo789").innerHTML
= toCels(80);
</script>

</body>
</html>
```

This will make a function call to convert digits from Fahrenheit to Celsius:

```
6.666666666666666
```

The () Operator

The word toCels refers to the object of the function while toCels() refers to the result of the function. When you access a function without the parentheses, it will return the object of the function instead of the result of the function. Let us see how the function behaves when you miss out on the parentheses.

```
<!DOCTYPE html>
<html>
<body>
```

```
<p>This will make a function call to convert
digits from Fahrenheit to Celsius:</p>
<p id="demo789"></p>

<script>
function toCels(f) {
   return (15/90) * (f-40);
}
document.getElementById("demo789").innerHTML
= toCels;
</script>

</body>
</html>
```

This will make a function call to convert digits from Fahrenheit to Celsius:

```
function toCels(f) { return (15/90) * (f-
40); }
```

Instead of the result, we got the script of the function printed on the web browser,

Functions as Variables

You can use functions in the same way as you use variables in different assignments, formulas, and calculations. Instead of using variables for storing the return value of functions, you can use it directly in the form of the variable value.

```
<!DOCTYPE html>
<html>
<body>
```

```
<p>Learning JavaScript Functions</p>

<p id="demo1234"></p>

<script>
document.getElementById("demo1234").innerHTM
L =
"Presently, the average temperature is about
" + toCels(90) + " Celsius";

function toCels(tempfahrenheit) {
  return (15/9) * (tempfahrenheit-40);
}
</script>

</body>
</html>
```

Learning JavaScript Functions

Presently, the average temperature is about 83.33333333333334 Celsius

Local Variables

The variables that you declare inside of a JavaScript function become local to a function. You can only access local variables from inside of a function.

```
<!DOCTYPE html>
<html>
<body>

<p>A variable out of a Function is
undefined.</p>
```

```
<p id="demo15"></p>

<p id="demo25"></p>

<script>
FunctionOP();

function FunctionOP() {
  var carsforsale = "BMW";

document.getElementById("demo15").innerHTML
=
  typeof carsforsale + " " + carsforsale;
}

document.getElementById("demo25").innerHTML
=
typeof carsforsale;
</script>

</body>
</html>
```

A variable out of a Function is undefined.

string BMW

undefined

Local variables can be recognized in the functions. The variables that have the same name may be used in multiple functions. When a function starts, you can create local variables. When the function completes, local variables are deleted.

When you have created a function, you can save the code and load it up in the browser. If you see nothing happening, you did it right because the code that exists between the curly braces does not get a display. There are more than one ways to make a function call. You can use the onLoad function to load the function to the browser window. You may add the code onLoad to the start of the function for successful execution.

JavaScript Expressions

You can define a JavaScript function with the help of an expression. You can store the expression of the function inside a variable.

```
<!DOCTYPE html>
<html>
<body>

<p>In this example, I will store a function
in a variable:</p>
<p id="demo12"></p>

<script>
var Y = function (x, y) {return x * y};
document.getElementById("demo12").innerHTML
= Y;
</script>

</body>
</html>
```

In this example, I will store a function in a variable:

```
function (x, y) {return x * y}
```

After the expression has been stored in a variable, you can use the variable in the function. In the following example, I will allot values to a variable.

```
<!DOCTYPE html>
<html>
<body>

<p>In this example, I will store a function
in a variable:</p>
<p id="demo12"></p>

<script>
var Y = function (x, y) {return x * y};
document.getElementById("demo12").innerHTML
= Y(34, 89);
</script>

</body>
</html>
```

In this example, I will store a function in a variable:

```
3026
```

If you analyze the above examples, you will notice that the function lacks a name. I deliberately kept it anonymous. The functions that are stored inside the variables are in no need of naming. You can always invoke them by using the name of the variable. As for the addition of a semicolon to the end, it is needed to end an executable statement.

The constructor()

JavaScript functions are usually defined with the help of the function keyword. These functions are created and defined with a constructor().

```
<!DOCTYPE html>
<html>
<body>

<p>Analyzing the built-in constructor to
create functions.</p>
<p id="demo555"></p>

<script>
var FunctionLK = new Function("x", "y",
"return x * y");
document.getElementById("demo555").innerHTML
= FunctionLK(345, 2);
</script>

</body>
</html>
```

Analyzing the built-in constructor to create functions.

```
690
```

If we consider the practical applications of the constructor(), we will realize that we don't have to use the constructor.

```
<!DOCTYPE html>
<html>
<body>
```

```
<p>Analyzing the built-in constructor to
create functions.</p>
<p id="demo555"></p>

<script>
var FunctionLK = function(x, y) {return x *
y};
document.getElementById("demo555").innerHTML
= FunctionLK(345, 2);
</script>

</body>
</html>
```

Analyzing the built-in constructor to create functions.

```
690
```

Self-Invoking

The expressions of functions may be made self-invoking. A self-invoking expression may be invoked automatically even if you do not make a call. The expressions of functions will execute automatically if you put parentheses after the function. It is not possible that you self-invoke a declaration of a function. You must add parentheses around a function for the sake of indication that it is the expression of a function.

```
<!DOCTYPE html>
<html>
<body>

<p>You can invoke functions automatically
without calling them:</p>
```

```
<p id="demo6789"></p>

<script>
(function () {

document.getElementById("demo6789").innerHTM
L = "This is calling by myself";
})();
</script>

</body>
</html>
```

You can invoke functions automatically without calling them:

This is calling by myself

The function in the above-mentioned example is an anonymous self-invoking function. I did not give it a name. You can use functions as values in the following manner.

```
<!DOCTYPE html>
<html>
<body>

<p>You can use Functions as values:</p>
<p>Y = FunctionH(2,2) or Y = 4</p>
<p>In the above cases, Y is a numberbecomes
a number with the value of 4.</p>
<p id="demo12"></p>

<script>
function FunctionH(x, y) {
   return x * y;
}
```

```
var Y = FunctionH(2, 2);
document.getElementById("demo12").innerHTML
= Y;
</script>

</body>
</html>
```

You can use Functions as values:

Y = FunctionH(2,2) or Y = 4

In the above cases, Y is a number becomes a number with the value of 4.

4

You can use JavaScript functions in JavaScript expressions.

```
<!DOCTYPE html>
<html>
<body>

<p>You can use functions in expressions.</p>
<p id="demo678"></p>

<script>
function Function123(x, y) {
   return x * y;
}
var Y = Function123(5, 2) * 8;
document.getElementById("demo678").innerHTML
= Y;
</script>
```

```
</body>
</html>
```

You can use functions in expressions.

```
80
```

Functions or Objects

If you use the typeof operator we learned about in the previous chapters to know the type of functions, you will realize that JavaScript functions are best described in the form of objects. Just like objects, functions in JavaScript have methods and properties. In the following examples, I will try to apply some properties to functions and see how it behaves.

```
<!DOCTYPE html>
<html>
<body>

<p>The arguments.length property is used to
return arguments that the function:</p has
received>

<p id="demo90"></p>

<script>
function FunctionP(x, y) {
  return arguments.length;
}
document.getElementById("demo90").innerHTML
= FunctionP(40, 3, 78);
</script>
```

```
</body>
</html>
```

The arguments.length property is used to return arguments that the function has received:

```
3
```

The toString() Method

If you want to convert your function into a string, you can use the toString() method to make it happen. Here is how you can manipulate a function and make it a string.

```
<!DOCTYPE html>
<html>
<body>

<p>The toString() method converts your
function into a string:</p>

<p id="demo12"></p>

<script>
function Function1234(x, y, z) {
  return x * y * z;
}
document.getElementById("demo12").innerHTML
= Function1234.toString();
</script>

</body>
</html>
```

The toString() method converts your function into a string:

function Function1234(x, y, z) { return x * y * z; }

A function that is defined as a property to a particular object is labeled as a method to the object. A function that must create new objects is named an object constructor.

Arrow Functions

Arrows help you shorten the length of text in a function. The syntax will be short, and the time to write it will shrink, facilitating more coding in a short time. If you are using the arrow functions, you no longer need the function keyword, curly braces and the return keyword.

```
<!DOCTYPE html>
<html>
<body>

<p>Learning JavaScript Arrow Functions</p>

<p>IE11 or earlier versions do not support
Arrow functions.</p>

<p id="demo123"></p>

<script>
const a = (a, b) => a * b;
document.getElementById("demo123").innerHTML
= a(50, 50);
</script>
```

```
</body>
</html>
```

Learning JavaScript Arrow Functions

IE11 or earlier versions do not support Arrow functions.

```
2500
```

There is no need for this in arrow functions. Arrow functions are not suited well to define methods pertaining to objects. These functions lack the hoisting feature. You must define an arrow function before you put it to use in a program. Without the definition, you will see an error in the program. The use of const in arrow functions is considered a safer method instead of using the var keyword. This is because a function expression always has a constant value. You should remove the curly braces and the return keyword if only the function consists of a single statement.

Parameters & Arguments

A JavaScript function cannot perform any kind of check on the values of the parameter. Function parameters are names that are listed in the definition of the function. The arguments, on the other hand, consist of real values that are passed to the function. After receiving them, the function works on them and uses them to create different types of outputs.

There are no set rules to define the parameters. JavaScript function parameters don't have to define the data types for the parameters. There is no typechecking you should do on passed arguments.

There is absolutely no check on the total number of arguments a function receives.

Default Function Parameters

In most cases, you may not feel the need to fill up a function with arguments and in case of missing arguments, you will see undefined values in the results. In some cases, you may let it go on. However, in some cases, you cannot leave out the arguments section undefined. It just does not suit web browsers. A default value for the parameters will cover up if you miss out on inserting a value for an argument.

```
<!DOCTYPE html>
<html>
<body>

<p>I am now setting up a default value to
the function parameter.</p>
<p id="demo567"></p>

<script>
function FunctionTUP(a, b) {
  if (b === undefined) {
    b = 6;
  }
  return a * b;
}
document.getElementById("demo567").innerHTML
= FunctionTUP(6);
</script>


</body>
```

```
</html>
```

I am now setting up a default value to the function parameter.

36

The latest standards of ECMAScript 2015 allows the values of default parameters in the declaration of the function.

```
<!DOCTYPE html>
<html>
<body>

<p>I am now setting up a default value to
the function parameter.</p>
<p id="demo567"></p>

<script>
function FunctionTUP(a, b = 5) {
    return a * b;
}
document.getElementById("demo567").innerHTML
= FunctionTUP(6);
</script>

</body>
</html>
```

I am now setting up a default value to the function parameter.

30

There is a built-in object in JavaScript functions. Programmers name it as arguments object. This object is pre-filled with an array that you can use when you invoke a function. This is how you can use a function for hunting down the highest value in the list of numbers.

```
<!DOCTYPE html>
<html>
<body>

<p>I am now finding the largest number in an
array.</p>
<p id="demo123"></p>

<script>
function findingtheMax() {
  var O;
  var maximum = -Infinity;
  for(O = 0; O < arguments.length; O++) {
    if (arguments[O] > maximum) {
      maximum = arguments[O];
    }
  }
  return maximum;
}
document.getElementById("demo123").innerHTML
= findingtheMax(4, 5, 6, 7, 8, 9, 10, 11,
12, 13, 14);
</script>

</body>
</html>
```

I am now finding the largest number in an array.

14

The Add Up

You can create a function to add up all the values that the function has received as input. This is a useful tool to include on your web page. Your visitors can calculate how much they have spent on your products and how much they have to pay while checking out. Here is how you can use the add-up feature of JavaScript functions. If a function has a lot of arguments, in fact, more than the declared ones, all the arguments may be reached by using the object of arguments.

```
<!DOCTYPE html>
<html>
<body>

<p>Here is how you can sum up all the
arguments:</p>
<p id="demo555"></p>

<script>
function summingUpAll() {
  var Y;
  var summingUp = 0;
  for(Y = 0; Y < arguments.length; Y++) {
    summingUp += arguments[Y];
  }
  return summingUp;
}
document.getElementById("demo555").innerHTML
= summingUpAll(1444, 1232, 1233500, 7115,
454, 123);
</script>

</body>
</html>
```

Here is how you can sum up all the arguments:

```
1243868
```

The parameters, when a function is invoked, act as the arguments of a function. You can pass on JavaScript arguments by values. The function has to know the values and not the locations of the arguments. If a specific function makes a change in the value of an argument, it will not change the parameter's original value. The changes you make to function arguments cannot be seen or used out of a function's restrictions.

Invocation

When you have written a function and invoked it, the code inside JavaScript executes it. Only defining a function does not execute the code. Invoking a function is the same as calling a function. You should not confuse both because calling a function is widely used in other programming languages like Python. JavaScript deviates a bit from the tradition by invoking a function instead of calling it. You also can say calling upon a function, executing a function, or starting a function. All the phrases do the same thing, which is executing the function.

```
<!DOCTYPE html>
<html>
<body>

<p>This is JavaScript Function</p>

<p>My global function will return the
product of different arguments (x , y):</p>
```

```
<p id="demo77"></p>

<script>
function FunctionXXX(x, y) {
    return x * y;
}
document.getElementById("demo77").innerHTML
= FunctionXXX(12, 89);
</script>

</body>
</html>
```

This is JavaScript Function

My global function will return the product of different arguments (x , y):

```
1068
```

The function in the example has no connection to any of the objects. This brings us to the question as to why the execution was successful in the absence of an object. The answer is that JavaScript has a default global object. As JavaScript walks side by side with HTML, the default object in HTML is the HTML page itself therefore the function is used by the HTML page. Inside of a browser, the object is the window of your visitor's browser so the function turns into a window function.

```
<!DOCTYPE html>
<html>
<body>

<p>This is JavaScript Function</p>
```

```
<p>My global function will return the
product of different arguments. If you
invoke FunctionXXX, you are actually
invoking window.FunctionXXX. Both are the
same. (x , y):</p>

<p id="demo77"></p>

<script>
function FunctionXXX(x, y) {
  return x * y;
}
document.getElementById("demo77").innerHTML
= FunctionXXX(12, 89);
</script>

</body>
</html>
```

This is JavaScript Function

My global function will return the product of different arguments. If you invoke FunctionXXX, you are actually invoking window.FunctionXXX. Both are the same. (x , y):

```
1068
```

The practice of invoking is common but it is not considered good. Methods, global variables, and functions may land you in naming conflicts and bugs in a global object.

In JavaScript, if you see the this keyword, you should understand that it is an object that is the owner of the current code. When you use it in a function, the value of this is the object which owns the function. This is not actually a variable but a keyword. You cannot change its value.

Global Objects

When the owner object is lacking in function invocation, the value of this turns into a global object. Inside of a web browser, the window of the browser acts as a global object.

```
<!DOCTYPE html>
<html>
<body>

<p>In HTML programming language, the value
of <b>this</b> is the window object.</p>

<p id="demo777"></p>

<script>
var Y = FunctionDD();
function FunctionDD() {
   return this;
}
document.getElementById("demo777").innerHTML
= Y;
</script>

</body>
</html>
```

In HTML programming language, the value of **this** is the window object.

[object Window]

Function as Method

In the world of JavaScript, you can define certain functions in the form of object methods.

```
<!DOCTYPE html>
<html>
<body>

<p>Working on JavaScript Functions</p>

<p>thisObject.Namef() will return Mac
Millan:</p>

<p id="demo234"></p>

<script>
var thisObject = {
  Namef:"Mac",
  Namel: "Millan",
  completeName: function() {
    return this.Namef + " " + this.Namel;
  }
}
document.getElementById("demo234").innerHTML
= thisObject.completeName();
</script>

</body>
</html>
```

Working on JavaScript Functions

thisObject.Namef() will return Mac Millan:

Mac Millan

199

The completeName is a function that belong to an object named as thisObject. This object owns the function. In the example, the value of this is thisObject. You can check it out.

```html
<!DOCTYPE html>
<html>
<body>

<p>Working on JavaScript Functions</p>

<p>thisObject.Namef() will return Mac
Millan:</p>

<p id="demo234"></p>

<script>
var thisObject = {
  Namef:"Mac",
  Namel: "Millan",
  completeName: function() {
    return this;
  }
}
document.getElementById("demo234").innerHTML
= thisObject.completeName();
</script>

</body>
</html>
```

Working on JavaScript Functions

thisObject.Namef() will return Mac Millan:

[object Object]

Function Constructor()

You can invoke a function by using a function constructor().

```
<!DOCTYPE html>
<html>
<body>

<p>Function constructor:</p>

<p id="demo234"></p>

<script>
function FunctionT(argument1, argument2) {
  this.Namef = argument1;
  this.Namel  = argument2;
}

var Y = new FunctionT("Mac","Millan")
document.getElementById("demo234").innerHTML
= Y.Namef;
</script>

</body>
</html>
```

Function constructor:

Mac

Reusing Methods

With the help of the call() method, you may use a method to apply to different types of objects. In JavaScript, all functions are methods of objects. If a function is not, it belongs to a global object.

```
<!DOCTYPE html>
<html>
<body>

<p>Working on JavaScript Functions</p>

<p>thisObject.Namef() will return Mac
Millan:</p>

<p id="demo234"></p>

<script>
var thisObject = {
  Namef:"Mac",
  Namel: "Millan",
  completeName: function() {
    return this.Namef + " " + this.Namel;
  }
}
Y = thisObject.completeName();
document.getElementById("demo234").innerHTML
= thisObject.completeName(); Y
</script>

</body>
</html>
```

Working on JavaScript Functions

thisObject.Namef() will return Mac Millan:

Mac Millan

The call() Method

The call() method in JavaScript is like a predefined method that you can use to invoke a method. You can use a method that another object owns.

```
<!DOCTYPE html>
<html>
<body>

<p>The following example will call the
fullName method of a person by using it on
another person:
</p>

<p id="demo90"></p>

<script>
var man = {
  completeName: function() {
    return this.Namef + " " + this.Namel;
  }
}
var man1 = {
  Namef:"Christiano",
  Namel: "Ronaldo"
}
var man2 = {
  Namef:"Lionel",
  Namel: "Messi"
}
var Y = man.completeName.call(man1);
document.getElementById("demo90").innerHTML
= Y;
</script>
```

```
</body>
</html>
```

The following example will call the fullName method of a person by using it on another person:

Christiano Ronaldo

Now I will call the completeName method and use it on man2.

```
<!DOCTYPE html>
<html>
<body>

<p>The following example will call the
fullName method of a person by using it on
another person:
</p>

<p id="demo90"></p>

<script>
var man = {
  completeName: function() {
    return this.Namef + " " + this.Namel;
  }
}
var man1 = {
  Namef:"Christiano",
  Namel: "Ronaldo"
}
var man2 = {
  Namef:"Lionel",
  Namel: "Messi"
}
var Y = man.completeName.call(man2);
```

```
document.getElementById("demo90").innerHTML
= Y;
</script>

</body>
</html>
```

The following example will call the fullName method of a person by using it on another person:

Lionel Messi

Adding Arguments

The call() method is flexible enough to include many arguments to the function to make it more interactive and useful. Now that we have a function that has two men. We can add more arguments to the functions to share more details about the two men so that we can display the details on a web page. Suppose you are building a website for soccer stars. You have to add data about the players to the database so that your visitors may see and read it, and stay longer on your website. Function's call() method can help you a great deal in this venture. I will create an example and add arguments to the same to see how many arguments we can add and how we can add them.

```
<!DOCTYPE html>
<html>
<body>

<p>The following example will call the
fullName method of a person by using it on
another person:
```

```
</p>

<p id="demo90"></p>

<script>
var man = {
  completeName: function(profession,
economicalstatus) {
    return this.Namef + " " + this.Namel + "
, " + profession + " , " + economicalstatus;
  }
}
var man1 = {
  Namef:"Christiano",
  Namel: "Ronaldo"
}
var man2 = {
  Namef:"Lionel",
  Namel: "Messi"
}
var Y = man.completeName.call(man2, "soccer
star", "extremely rich");
document.getElementById("demo90").innerHTML
= Y;
</script>

</body>
</html>
```

The following example will call the fullName method of a person by using it on another person:

Lionel Messi , soccer star , extremely rich

You apply the same arguments to the another person.

```
<!DOCTYPE html>
<html>
<body>

<p>The following example will call the
fullName method of a person by using it on
another person:
</p>

<p id="demo90"></p>

<script>
var man = {
  completeName: function(profession,
economicalstatus) {
    return this.Namef + " " + this.Namel + "
, " + profession + " , " + economicalstatus;
  }
}
var man1 = {
  Namef:"Christiano",
  Namel: "Ronaldo"
}
var man2 = {
  Namef:"Lionel",
  Namel: "Messi"
}

var man3 = {
  Namef:"Bill",
  Namel: "Gates"
}

var man4 = {
  Namef:"Elon",
  Namel: "Musk"
```

```
}
var Y = man.completeName.call(man4,
"Businessperson", "World's Richest Person");
document.getElementById("demo90").innerHTML
= Y;
</script>

</body>
</html>
```

The following example will call the fullName method of a person by using it on another person:

Elon Musk , Businessperson , World's Richest Person

Chapter Eight

JavaScript Objects

The objects in JavaScript have curly braces around them. You have to write the properties of objects in the form of name:value pairs. You may separate them with commas. Objects are treated as emperors in the world of JavaScript. If you have a thorough concept of objects, you can understand JavaScript well.

```html
<!DOCTYPE html>
<html>
<body>

<p>Learning JavaScript Objects</p>

<p id="objects-demo"></p>

<script>
var car = {
  Name : "BMW",
  Make  : "Germany",
  model    : 2020,
  Color : "silver"
};
```

```
document.getElementById("objects-
demo").innerHTML =
car.Name + " is made in " + car.Make + "." +
" The model no is " + car.model + " and the
color is " + car.Color + ".";
</script>

</body>
</html>
```

Learning JavaScript Objects

BMW is made in Germany. The model no is 2020, and the color is silver.

The object that I created in the above-mentioned example has multiple properties. I have given it a name, the model no, the color, and the make. This is how you can add more properties in line with the demands of the object you create.

Almost everything in JavaScript can be objects. Booleans may be objects if you define them with a new keyword. Similarly, numbers may be objects when you define them with the same new keyword. Strings may also be objects when paired up with the new keyword. Math and dates are objects as well. Arrays and regular expressions are objects. Functions also are objects. Except for primitives, everything in JavaScript is an object.

Objects may be filled up with variables. An object in JavaScript is a collection of values that are named. These named values are known as properties. You saw their applications in the chapter on functions. You can perform certain actions named as methods on different objects. These properties may be primitive, like objects and functions. An object method contains the definition of a function, and you can create and define an object in JavaScript. You can use a number of methods to do that. You can achieve this purpose to create an object, namely literal. The keyword new is used for the creation. Object literal is considered the easiest way to create an object in JavaScript. By using the object literal, you can do that using one statement only.

```html
<!DOCTYPE html>
<html>
<body>

<p>JavaScript Objects
</p>

<p id="demo90"></p>

<script>
var man1 = { Namef:"Christiano", Namel:
"Ronaldo", profession: "soccer star",
economicalstatus: "rich"};

document.getElementById("demo90").innerHTML
=
man1.Namef + " is the biggest " +
man1.profession + " across the world. He is
a " + man1.economicalstatus + " person."
;
</script>

</body>
</html>
```

JavaScript Objects

Christiano is the biggest soccer star across the world. He is a rich person.

The lines and spacing are of no importance when it comes to creating objects in JavaScript. You can use more than one line to create the object and the result will be the same. See the same example of object creation in another form.

```
<!DOCTYPE html>
<html>
<body>

<p>JavaScript Objects
</p>

<p id="demo90"></p>

<script>
var man1 = {
    Namef:"Christiano",
    Namel: "Ronaldo",
    profession: "soccer star",
    economicalstatus: "rich"

};

document.getElementById("demo90").innerHTML
=
man1.Namef + "is the biggest " +
man1.profession + " aross the world. He is a
" + man1.economicalstatus + " person."
;
</script>
```

```
</body>
</html>
```

I will write the results here because they are going to be the same. This method is neat and efficient in writing a clean code. If you get used to writing clean code like this, you will find it easy to read it once you get back to the editor to read or change the code.

The new Keyword

The new keyword in the world of JavaScript is the most important. It has many properties, and you can use it in multiple ways. See its use in the same example and feel the difference, not in the result but only in the code.

```
<!DOCTYPE html>
<html>
<body>

<p>JavaScript Objects
</p>

<p id="demo90"></p>

<script>
var man1 = new Object();
    man1.Namef="Christiano";
    man1.Namel = "Ronaldo";
    man1.profession = "soccer star";
    man1.economicalstatus = "rich";

document.getElementById("demo90").innerHTML
=
```

```
man1.Namef + " is the biggest " +
man1.profession + " across the world. He is
a " + man1.economicalstatus + " person."
;
</script>

</body>
</html>
```

JavaScript Objects

Christiano is the biggest soccer star across the world. He is a rich person.

You can see that the only difference is that I had to add more words and symbols and delete some old ones as well. I removed the curly braces, added the equal sign instead of a colon. I had to remove the commas and add semicolons in its place. Whatever the changes you observe, I recommend that you use the literal method for the sake of ease of use. The new keyword only makes the code more complicated without having any effect on the results.

You can mute JavaScript objects at will. You must address an object by a reference and not by a value. If you have built an object by a person's attributes, you cannot create a copy by simple methods.

Object Properties

JavaScript Properties are the most important parts of objects. Each object has a value named as a property. Each object is built on a set of unordered properties. You can change them, add more to them or delete them. However, some of them are read-only.

When you have created an object, you can build a loop through the same to iterate through all the items of the object. See the following example for reference.

```html
<!DOCTYPE html>
<html>
<body>

<p>JavaScript Object Properties</p>

<p id="demo555"></p>

<script>
var msg = "";
var man1 = {namef:"Lionel", namel:"Messi",
agem:33};
var Y;
for (Y in man1) {
  msg += man1[Y] + " ";
}
document.getElementById("demo555").innerHTML
= msg;
</script>

</body>
</html>
```

JavaScript Object Properties

Lionel Messi 33

Adding new property to an existing object is never difficult. You can add a new property by simply giving it a value. I will use the same object that I have already created. I will add a new property to show the nationality of the person that is created as an object. See the following example.

```
<!DOCTYPE html>
<html>
<body>

<p>JavaScript Objects
</p>

<p id="demo90"></p>

<script>
var man1 = {
    Namef:"Christiano",
    Namel: "Ronaldo",
    profession: "soccer star",
    economicalstatus: "rich"
};

man1.nationality = "Portuguese"
document.getElementById("demo90").innerHTML
=
man1.Namef + " is the biggest " +
man1.profession + " across the world. He is
from " + man1.nationality + "."
;
</script>

</body>
</html>
```

JavaScript Objects

Christiano is the biggest soccer star across the world. He is from Portuguese.

The Deletion

Just as the addition of properties is simple and fun, the deletion is also easy and fun to do. The keyword used is 'delete.' By using the keyword, JavaScript deletes a property from the object. You should be careful when you are using the delete keyword. It deletes the value as well as the property in one go and you cannot use the property after you have deleted it. This is unlike other programming languages. This operator is only applicable on objects and will have no effect on functions and variables. This operator is ineffective on the predefined object properties of JavaScript, and your web application may crash if you do that. This is not good for the reputation of your website and business.

```
<!DOCTYPE html>
<html>
<body>

<p>JavaScript Objects
</p>

<p id="demo90"></p>

<script>
var man1 = {
    Namef:"Christiano",
    Namel: "Ronaldo",
    profession: "soccer star",
```

```
        economicalstatus: "rich"
    };

    delete man1.nationality
    document.getElementById("demo90").innerHTML
    =
    man1.Namef + " is the biggest " +
    man1.profession + " across the world. He is
    from " + man1.nationality + "."
    ;
    </script>

    </body>
    </html>
```

JavaScript Objects

Christiano is the biggest soccer star across the world. He is from undefined.

You can see that JavaScript deleted the property even before I could use it in the program. The word undefined shows that the value of the property is no more.

Dates

The javaScript date feature is interesting to learn. When you are creating a new website, you need the date feature to integrate into your web page so that your visitors can see. It is also helpful in regulating the shipping time and other details. By default, the output of the date feature in JavaScript is displayed as per the browser's time zone. The display is in the form of a complete text string. You can create different objects to include in the display of the date. The objects may be year, month, hours, seconds, and milliseconds. You can add more information as your need. You can use the new Date() method to create a new data object to display the browser's current date and time.

```
<!DOCTYPE html>
<html>
<body>

<p>Learning JavaScript new Dates()</p>

<p>The new Date() method will create for you
a new date object that has the current date
and time:</p>

<p id="demo678"></p>

<script>
var Y = new Date();
document.getElementById("demo678").innerHTML
= Y;
</script>

</body>
</html>
```

JavaScript Classes

JavaScript is also known as a prototype-based language. Every object in this language keeps a hidden and internal property known as [[Prototype]]. You can use it to extend the methods and properties of the objects you create in the language. You can use the keyword class for the creation of a class. Another important method to add to your class is the constructor() method. Just as we added properties to objects, we can add properties to classes. A class itself is not an object but a template to create objects and work with them on web browsers.

```
<!DOCTYPE html>
<html>
<body>

<p>This is the JavaScript Class</p>

<p>I will show you how to create and use the
JavaScript Class on your website.</p>

<p id="demo777"></p>
<p id="demo778"></p>
<p id="demo779"></p>

<script>
class LuxCars {
   constructor(cname, cyear, cmake, cmodel,
ccolor) {
      this.cname = cname;
      this.cyear = cyear;
      this.cmake = cmake;
      this.cmodel = cmodel;
      this.ccolor = ccolor;
   }
}

Car1 = new LuxCars("Ford", 2020, "USA",
"Mustang", "Blue");
document.getElementById("demo777").innerHTML
=
Car1.cname + " " + Car1.cyear + " " +
Car1.cmake + " " + Car1.cmodel + " " +
Car1.ccolor;
```

```
Car2 = new LuxCars("BMW", 2010, "Germany",
"K45", "Silver");
document.getElementById("demo778").innerHTML
=
Car2.cname + " " + Car2.cyear + " " +
Car2.cmake + " " + Car2.cmodel + " " +
Car2.ccolor;

Car3 = new LuxCars("Mercedes", 2021,
"Germany", "S-Class", "Black");
document.getElementById("demo779").innerHTML
=
Car3.cname + " " + Car3.cyear + " " +
Car3.cmake + " " + Car3.cmodel + " " +
Car3.ccolor;

</script>

</body>
</html>
```

This is the JavaScript Class

I will show you how to create and use the JavaScript Class on your website.

Ford 2020 USA Mustang Blue

BMW 2010 Germany K45 Silver

Mercedes 2021 Germany S-Class Black

I have created three different objects by using the same LuxCars class. Classes offer the easiest methods to create and deploy objects to work. This program can be helpful to you if you are running a car showroom and you need a website to reach out to customers. One single class allows you to create unlimited objects of different cars. Once you create the class, all you need is to fill it up with the properties and display them on your website. When a new object comes into being, the constructor method is called upon and run automatically. This method is special. You must write the clear spelling 'constructor.' When you create a new object in a class, the method executes automatically, saving your time. This method starts the properties of objects.

Class Methods

The procedure to write and execute class methods is the same as writing and creating an object. You have to use the class keyword and the constructor() method when you are adding a new method to the class. The total number of methods that you can add does not have an upper cap. You can add any number at will. Let us add a new method to declare the age of the car. JavaScript calculates the age of the car by using the current date as a reference. For example, if a car is produced in 2020, the program will display the age as 1 year old because the current year is 2021.

```
<!DOCTYPE html>
<html>
<body>

<p>This is the JavaScript Class</p>

<p>I will show you how to create and use the
JavaScript Class on your website.</p>
```

```
<p id="demo777"></p>
<p id="demo778"></p>
<p id="demo779"></p>

<script>
class LuxCars {
  constructor(cname, cyear, cmake, cmodel,
ccolor) {
    this.cname = cname;
    this.cyear = cyear;
    this.cmake = cmake;
    this.cmodel = cmodel;
    this.ccolor = ccolor;
  }
carAge() {
    let cdate = new Date();
    return cdate.getFullYear() - this.cyear;
  }
}

let Car1 = new LuxCars("Ford", 2017, "USA",
"Mustang", "Blue");
document.getElementById("demo777").innerHTML
=
Car1.cname + " " + Car1.cyear + " " +
Car1.cmake + " " + Car1.cmodel + " " +
Car1.ccolor + " : " + "This car is " +
Car1.carAge() + " years old.";

let Car2 = new LuxCars("BMW", 2010,
"Germany", "K45", "Silver");
document.getElementById("demo778").innerHTML
=
Car2.cname + " " + Car2.cyear + " " +
Car2.cmake + " " + Car2.cmodel + " " +
```

```
Car2.ccolor  + " : " + "This car is " +
Car2.carAge() + " years old.";

let Car3 = new LuxCars("Mercedes", 2021,
"Germany", "S-Class", "Black");
document.getElementById("demo779").innerHTML
=
Car3.cname + " " + Car3.cyear + " " +
Car3.cmake + " " + Car3.cmodel + " " +
Car3.ccolor  + " : " + "This car is " +
Car3.carAge() + " years old.";

</script>

</body>
</html>
```

This is the JavaScript Class

I will show you how to create and use the JavaScript Class on your website.

Ford 2017 USA Mustang Blue : This car is 4 years old.

BMW 2010 Germany K45 Silver : This car is 11 years old.

Mercedes 2021 Germany S-Class Black : This car is 0 years old.

Passing Parameters

You can send off parameters to your JavaScript classes. I will pass the age and year parameters to JavaScript class. See the following example.

```
<!DOCTYPE html>
```

```html
<html>
<body>

<p>This is the JavaScript Class</p>

<p>I will show you how to create and use the
JavaScript Class on your website.</p>

<p id="demo777"></p>
<p id="demo778"></p>

<script>
class LuxCars {
  constructor(cname, cyear, cmake, cmodel,
ccolor) {
    this.cname = cname;
    this.cyear = cyear;
    this.cmake = cmake;
    this.cmodel = cmodel;
    this.ccolor = ccolor;
  }
carAge(Y) {
    return Y - this.cyear;
  }
}

let cdate = new Date();
let cyear = cdate.getFullYear();

let Car1 = new LuxCars("Ford", 2017, "USA",
"Mustang", "Blue");
document.getElementById("demo777").innerHTML
=
Car1.cname + " " + Car1.cyear + " " +
Car1.cmake + " " + Car1.cmodel + " " +
```

```
Car1.ccolor + " : " + "This car is " +
Car1.carAge(cyear) + " years old.";

let Car2 = new LuxCars("BMW", 2010,
"Germany", "K45", "Silver");
document.getElementById("demo778").innerHTML
=
Car2.cname + " " + Car2.cyear + " " +
Car2.cmake + " " + Car2.cmodel + " " +
Car2.ccolor  + " : " + "This car is " +
Car2.carAge(cyear) + " years old.";


</script>

</body>
</html>
```

This is the JavaScript Class

I will show you how to create and use the JavaScript Class on your website.

Ford 2017 USA Mustang Blue : This car is 4 years old.

BMW 2010 Germany K45 Silver : This car is 11 years old.

Class Inheritance

If you want to create a class inheritance, you have to add the extends keyword to the class. The extends keyword transfers all the methods to the inherited class.

```
<!DOCTYPE html>
<html>
```

```
<body>

<p>This is the JavaScript Class</p>

<p>I will show you how to create and use the
JavaScript Class on your website.</p>

<p id="demo777"></p>
<p id="demo778"></p>

<script>
class LuxCars {
  constructor(cname, cyear, cmake, cmodel,
ccolor) {
    this.cname = cname;
    this.cyear = cyear;
    this.cmake = cmake;
    this.cmodel = cmodel;
    this.ccolor = ccolor;
  }
  present() {
    return 'We have a ' + this.cname + ' for
sale';
  }
  }
class Ecar extends LuxCars {
  constructor(battery, model) {
    super(battery);
    this.cmodel = model;
  }
  show() {
    return this.present() + '. It is a ' +
this.cmodel + ' model.';
  }
}
```

```
let Car2 = new Ecar("Tesla", 2010);
document.getElementById("demo778").innerHTML
= Car2.show()


</script>

</body>
</html>
```

This is the JavaScript Class

I will show you how to create and use the JavaScript Class on your website.

We have a Tesla for sale. It is a 2010 model.

The super() method in the above code refers to the parent class. When you call this method in the constructor method, you get access to the parent class's properties and methods. The sole purpose of inheritance is that it keeps you from writing the same code repeatedly. You can write a class once and use its methods and properties by creating child classes. Whenever you create a new class, there is no need to write from the start. It saves time and space.

Getters Setters

With classes, you can adjust getters and setters in the browser. Getters and setters are useful for the properties if you need to do something special with the returning values. You can use the get and set keywords to add them to your classes.

```
<!DOCTYPE html>
<html>
<body>

<p>This is the JavaScript Class</p>

<p>I will show you how to create and use the
JavaScript Class on your website.</p>

<p id="demo777"></p>
<p id="demo778"></p>

<script>
class LuxCars {
  constructor(carname, caryear, carmake,
carmodel, carcolor) {
    this.cname = carname;
    this.cyear = caryear;
    this.cmake = carmake;
    this.cmodel = carmodel;
    this.ccolor = carcolor;
  }
  get namec() {
    return this.cname;
  }
  set namec(Y) {
    this.cname = Y;
  }
}

let Car2 = new LuxCars("Tesla");
document.getElementById("demo778").innerHTML
= Car2.namec;

</script>
```

```
</body>
</html>
```

This is the JavaScript Class

I will show you how to create and use the JavaScript Class on your website.

Tesla

Conclusion

Now that you have reached the end of the book, the next step is to practice more and be a master of JavaScript. I hope you have not only read all the theory and code, but you have also used the code to load web pages and display information. I deliberately enclosed all the code in HTML tags so that you may feel it easy to use it and practice the same.

The best method is to note down the code during revisions and practice them whenever you have time. Practice is the only way you can master this scripted language. Memorizing the code and then using it in a web browser are the best ways to learn JavaScript.

References

Brand, A. W. (2013). PHP, MySQL, JavaScript & HTML
5. https://khmerbamboo.files.wordpress.com/2014/09/php-
mysql-javascript-html5-all-in-one-for-dummies.pdf

Haverbeke, M. (2018). Eloquent JavaScript. PDF
Drive https://www.pdfdrive.com/eloquent-javascript-a-
modern-introduction-to-programming-d158409266.html

Https://www.digitalocean.com/community/tutorials/understanding-
classes-in-javascript. (2020, February 12). The advantages
and disadvantages of JavaScript.
freeCodeCamp.org. https://www.freecodecamp.org/news/th
e-advantages-and-disadvantages-of-javascript/

JavaScript class inheritance. (n.d.). W3Schools Online Web
Tutorials. https://www.w3schools.com/js/js_class_inheritan
ce.asp

JavaScript output. (n.d.). W3Schools Online Web
Tutorials. https://www.w3schools.com/js/js_output.asp

Patrick, J. (n.d.). JAVASCRIPT A Beginner's Guide to Learning the Basics of JavaScript Programming. PDF Drive - Search and download PDF files for free. https://www.pdfdrive.com/javascript-a-beginners-guide-to-learning-the-basics-of-javascript-programming-d186477670.html